CAMBRIDGE LIBRARY COLLECTION

Books of enduring scholarly value

Anthropology

The first use of the word 'anthropology' in English was recorded in 1593, but its modern use to indicate the study and science of humanity became current in the late nineteenth century. At that time a separate discipline had begun to evolve from many component strands (including history, archaeology, linguistics, biology and anatomy), and the study of so-called 'primitive' peoples was given impetus not only by the reports of individual explorers but also by the need of colonial powers to define and classify the unfamiliar populations which they governed. From the ethnographic writings of early explorers to the 1898 Cambridge expedition to the Torres Straits, often regarded as the first truly 'anthropological' field research, these books provide eye-witness information on often vanished peoples and ways of life, as well as evidence for the development of a new scientific discipline.

Desert and Water Gardens of the Red Sea

Cyril Crossland (1878-1943) was Director of the Sudan Pearl Fishery between 1905 and 1922. At this time, the British colonial government had taken charge of running the fishery, with local fishermen as employees. A marine biologist and zoologist, Crossland was praised in his obituary in the journal *Nature* as 'one of the last explorer-naturalists of the Darwin type'. This book is both an account of his life in the Sudan and a scientific survey of the coral reefs on the Red Sea coast. It offers a lively description of the region, its people and customs, and a clear, accessible explanation of the development of coral reefs. In Crossland's time this region had not been fully mapped by Western explorers and this study was an important contribution to knowledge. The book is illustrated with many of Crossland's own photographs of landscapes and people and his diagrams of the coral reefs.

T0370669

Cambridge University Press has long been a pioneer in the reissuing of out-of-print titles from its own backlist, producing digital reprints of books that are still sought after by scholars and students but could not be reprinted economically using traditional technology. The Cambridge Library Collection extends this activity to a wider range of books which are still of importance to researchers and professionals, either for the source material they contain, or as landmarks in the history of their academic discipline.

Drawing from the world-renowned collections in the Cambridge University Library, and guided by the advice of experts in each subject area, Cambridge University Press is using state-of-the-art scanning machines in its own Printing House to capture the content of each book selected for inclusion. The files are processed to give a consistently clear, crisp image, and the books finished to the high quality standard for which the Press is recognised around the world. The latest print-on-demand technology ensures that the books will remain available indefinitely, and that orders for single or multiple copies can quickly be supplied.

The Cambridge Library Collection will bring back to life books of enduring scholarly value (including out-of-copyright works originally issued by other publishers) across a wide range of disciplines in the humanities and social sciences and in science and technology.

Desert and Water Gardens of the Red Sea

Being an Account of the Natives and the Shore Formations of the Coast

Cyril Crossland

CAMBRIDGE
UNIVERSITY PRESS

CAMBRIDGE UNIVERSITY PRESS

Cambridge, New York, Melbourne, Madrid, Cape Town, Singapore,
São Paolo, Delhi, Dubai, Tokyo, Mexico City

Published in the United States of America by Cambridge University Press, New York

www.cambridge.org
Information on this title: www.cambridge.org/9781108016018

This edition first published 1913
This digitally printed version 2010

ISBN 978-1-108-01601-8 Paperback

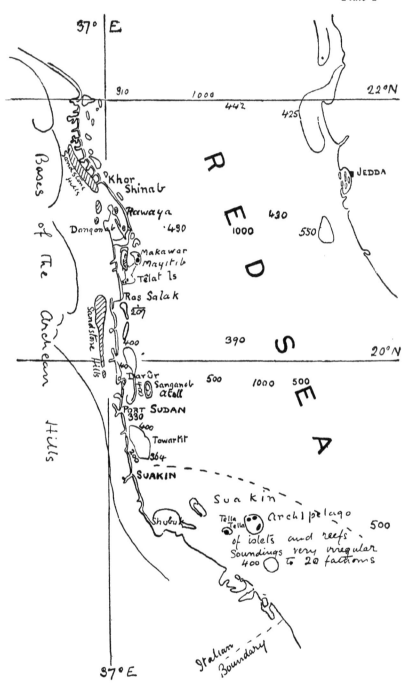

Plate I

Fig. 1. Coast of the Anglo-Egyptian Sudan

Sandstone hills shaded, *small* islands black. Coastline double, the outer line being the edge of the fringing reef. The thin lines enclosing roughly oval or elongated areas at sea are the barrier reefs. Figures on sea represent depths in fathoms.

DESERT AND WATER GARDENS
OF THE RED SEA

CAMBRIDGE UNIVERSITY PRESS
London: FETTER LANE, E.C.
C. F. CLAY, Manager

Edinburgh: 100, PRINCES STREET
London: WILLIAM WESLEY & SON, 28, ESSEX STREET, STRAND
Berlin: A. ASHER AND CO.
Leipzig: F. A. BROCKHAUS
New York: G. P. PUTNAM'S SONS
Bombay and Calcutta: MACMILLAN AND CO., Ltd.

Plate III

Fig. 3. A sandstorm seen from among the Barrier Reefs

DESERT AND WATER GARDENS

OF THE

RED SEA

BEING AN ACCOUNT OF THE NATIVES AND THE
SHORE FORMATIONS OF THE COAST

BY

CYRIL CROSSLAND

M.A. Cantab., B.Sc. Lond., F.L.S., F.Z.S.

Marine Biologist to the Sudan Government

Cambridge:

at the University Press

1913

𝕮𝖆𝖒𝖇𝖗𝖎𝖉𝖌𝖊:

PRINTED BY JOHN CLAY, M.A.

AT THE UNIVERSITY PRESS

TO MY WIFE

TO WHOSE BRAVE ENDURANCE OF A LARGE
SHARE OF MY EXILE IS OWING MUCH
OF WHATEVER I HAVE ACHIEVED, OR
OF WHAT SUCCESS MAY YET BE MINE

PREFACE

IT is my fortune to know intimately a portion of the Red Sea coast, that between 18° N. and 22° N. on the western side. This must be one of the least known coastlines of the world. Until 1905, the Admiralty Chart shewed an area of 25 square miles of reef, which the surveys run for the approaches to the new town of Port Sudan have proved to be non-existent. Though a considerable distance north of this point has now been accurately surveyed, practically no details of the great barrier system of reefs leading up to the Rawaya Peninsula, or of the land inside the coastline, have yet been mapped.

As I shall shew later, certain features of the maritime plain are of the greatest interest, but they have only been hurriedly examined by Mr Dunn, one of the Sudan Government geologists ; and no survey of the country has yet been made.

The explanation is not to be found in any laxity in either the Admiralty or the Sudan Government surveyors. Considering that the country is an absolutely unproductive desert, traversed only by a sparse population of nomads, that no steamer passes within miles of the outermost reefs, that the native vessels sail by perhaps at the rate of one a month, the existing chart is a monument to the greatness of the Admiralty's conception of taking the whole world for its province, even the most useless desert coasts.

Perhaps the fact that this country, though so near to Europe, is only artificially made habitable at all, may add interest to my account; but besides the description of things and peoples more or less unique and peculiar to this country, I have aimed at giving information of general interest. For instance, in treating of the coral reefs I describe features of the barrier system which may be unique in the world, but I have combined with the description of this special point a general account of coral animals and the reefs which they build. This may recall and complete the interesting conversations I have had on such subjects with friends both at home and in those places where the very streets and houses were once parts of coral reefs.

Biologists have one way of justifying their existence which has to some extent been neglected. Their reply to the eternal question "What good is it? where does the money come in?" should be, in some cases, that of the artist. Just as there are those to whom the love of beauty in pictures, sculpture and architecture is one of the things in life they would least wish to lose, to whom the existence of professional artists is more than justified, so there are many outside the ranks of professional biologists, to whom the romance of the beginnings of life, and of strange lowly forms of being, might become an absorbing interest, an enrichment of life in which money does not necessarily "come in" at all.

This is an interest especially accessible to the exiles of the coral seas, where ordinary amusements are so restricted that their repetition produces a sense of loneliness and monotony scarcely conceivable by the man of normal surroundings. For these among my friends I have written, beginning from the beginning and omitting as not pertinent to the questions they ask me, many points vital to the science of animal anatomy, but not essential to their understanding perfectly such questions as, "What is the coral organism? How does it build up these rocks?"

These questions are my own special province, I deal with them as an expert though writing so briefly, but in the rest of the book I have made no attempt at writing a treatise on anthropology or a guide book to the Sudan coast, but only to present what is to me beautiful, interesting or amusing in the places and people as I see them. What I describe I write of with all the accuracy of which my words are capable ; so far as it goes, all is strictly true. But alas, no one has yet written of the beauty of this desert coast as it should be written. Could I describe one half the beauty of the memory pictures I owe to this country, I should be a poet, whereas I am only a man of facts.

I wonder much at the neglect of this route through the Red Sea by those who make extended journeys on the Nile. From Atbara a perfectly comfortable train journey carries one swiftly through desert and mountains to either Port Sudan or Suakin. I trust that I have written clearly enough to prove that a few days on this coast is time well spent.

Finally, this route to Khartum and Uganda is a quicker and cheaper one than that by the Nile.

Prof. J. Stanley Gardiner's reading and criticism of what follows is but one of many kindnesses, and is especially valuable in the case of the chapters on corals and reefs, of which our knowledge has been so greatly added to by Prof. Gardiner's researches.

CYRIL CROSSLAND.

WINDERMERE,
   September 1912.

POSTSCRIPT TO PREFACE

ON reading my book for the press I find that it has a moral, a thing never intended! It is that real romance and beauty are to be found in things as they are, so that the man of science, popularly supposed to be hardened by "materialistic" pursuits, has opportunities for a truer worship than has the sentimentalist who bows before idols of his own imagination.

I tender my thanks to the Council of the Linnean Society who have permitted the reproduction of most of the illustrations of Chapter IX and some of those of Chapter VIII from my papers in their *Journal*, vol. xxxi, in which the account of Red Sea Structure was originally published for Scientific readers, and to Messrs Murray and the Challenger Society for the use of two diagrams from their *Science of the Sea*. The beautiful photograph of a Suakin mosque is by my friend W. H. Lake, Esq.

CYRIL CROSSLAND.

Dongonab, Red Sea.
Sept. 1913.

CONTENTS

PART I

THE DESERT AND ITS PEOPLE

Contents

PART II

CORALS AND CORAL REEFS

CHAPTER VII

CORALS AND CORAL ANIMALS

CHAPTER VIII

THE BUILDING OF REEFS

CHAPTER IX

THE MAKING OF THE RED SEA

LIST OF ILLUSTRATIONS, ETC.

ERRATA

p. 88. *For* Hydniopora *read* Hydnopora.

p. 120. Halaib is a name unknown to natives, who call the place Olê. From this the official name is derived through Arab orthography probably. The Arabic alphabet is the best possible for its own language, and the worst for any other.

PART I

CHAPTER I

THE SUDAN COAST

In thinking of an unknown place it is inevitable that some image should rise in the mind and recur until it is finally shattered by the revelation of its almost total falsity which a visit to that country brings about. My own imaginings, based on what I had seen in passing through the Red Sea on my way to Zanzibar, were fantastically unreal. I saw blue mountain tops like jagged teeth appearing over the horizon at sunset, and combining these with what I had seen of the reefs and islands of the Gulf of Suez and Bab-el-Mandeb, it came as a shock, some years later, to find that the essential of life on the coast is the great maritime plain, the mountains remaining in the distance, still inaccessible for me.

My first actual sight of the country was typical of the cloudy weather which sometimes occurs in winter. Our little steamer was entering the great gap in the barrier reefs five miles out to sea, directly opposite to what is now the harbour of Port Sudan. Then it was only "Mersa Shêkh Barûd[1]," a saint's tomb forming the only work of man for many miles. Grey sea and sky, blue mountains, faintly visible beyond the great dull plain, greeted me ; later, the little tomb, built on a knoll of yellow coral rock at the entrance of the inlet, a mark for sailors, gleamed white out of all this greyness. Coming nearer still, one saw that the shore is composed of a low level line of yellowish cliffs, about six feet high, undermined below by the constant wash of the waves and sloping inwards at

---

[1] For the story of Shêkh Barûd's death see p. 37.

their summits. The shore is separated from the blue-black water by a broad band of green shallows, its outer edge defined by a thin white line of breakers. This is the edge of the fringing reef, which is practically uniform and continuous through the length of both shores of the Red Sea. We were sailing in a channel of fairly deep water partially protected from the waves of the open sea by the barrier reefs. These are a series of shoals and surface reefs, extending parallel to the shore, at a distance of one to five miles out to sea.

This, my first view of the country, may be taken as typical of the whole coast, variations in its uniformity being few. The weather that day was rather exceptional, for often in winter there is all the incomparable sparkle of sunshine and crisp breeze of Egypt, and the mountains, in this wonderful air, come nearer. There are days when I have seen distinctly all the light and shade of their precipices 80 miles away. I leave to your imagination the clearness, almost brilliance, of the great mountains seen at only 15 miles on such days as these. Even so they do not lose their dignity of form and distance, while revealing their vast precipices and terrible ravines, all bare rock, no vegetation, or even soil, to soften their outlines. Truly they are a "great and terrible wilderness." So too is the plain, vast and uniform, all open to the sky—neither the few acacia bushes[1], nor the sparse tufts of apparently dead and almost woody grass serving to render it soft and pleasant to the eye, nor to cover its grey sand and gravel from scorching in the rays of the sun. Great and terrible, a naked savage land, every feature typifying thirst and starvation, so it became to me during my first visit. I was glad indeed to leave, half hoping I should never return.

In absence savagery and poverty faded, and I found myself picturing the mountains at sunrise, ruddy clear, the peacock blue of the deep sea with white waves, the light blues, greens, yellows, and browns of the coral reefs and the submarine gardens they shelter, and so back again to the

[1] *Acacia tortilis.*

mountains at evening, veiled now in the tender blues and purples of our hills at home, but behind them sunsets of indescribable magnificence. To memory came back that great plain, its openness, its sense of freedom wild as the sea itself, which indeed once gave it birth. I thought of how after a little winter rain there comes the spring; the sand is dotted with little flowers, weeds elsewhere perhaps, here brave conquerors of the desert; the shallow watercourses are full of grass. The acacia bushes become a tender green with a moss-like growth of tiny curling leaves giving out the sweetest of scents, recalling our larches at home. Later they are covered with flowers, like little balls of scented down on slender stalks.

Two of those transiently appearing plants, amongst the commonest of all, have special claims. One, the little "forget-me-not" of the desert, is loved individually for its pure white flowers, the other, for its effects when growing in mass. This latter has a peculiar form, a network of branches springing from a central stem, spread out horizontally over the sand, bearing cylindrical bright green leaves and tiny yellow flowers. The whole plant is of great delicacy, and would be unnoticed by the non-botanical observer but that it is sometimes so abundant as to carpet the ground like a bright green moss, which later is golden from the abundance of its tiny flowers. At the approach of summer, the heat of which has an effect like a touch of frost in England, its leaves take on splendid autumn tints. Once I landed on an islet circled with the low grey-green bushes always present on sand islands, within which I found a display of colour the beauty of which will enrich my store of memory pictures for the rest of my life. The principal scheme was a golden carpet of these tiny, almost microscopic flowers merging into a bright and tender green, and on to all kinds of orange browns and reds. Here and there another of the plants of this peculiar salt-loving flora gave patches of wonderful deep crimson. These vivid colours were thrown up by the dull grey green of the encircling bushy plants, which remain the same all the year round, and by clumps of a "grass[1]" which is of a deep glossy green colour like that of rushes, the whole being in a shallow depression in the dull yellow coral rock. All the transient beauty of changing bracken, moss, and heather was here, but with a wonderful quality of translucence under that blazing sun. As a background to all this imagine the bluest of blue seas and mountains seen over the water, and the picture is complete.

The only really conspicuous flower of the coast lands is a *Pancratium*, a bulb-plant with pure white delicately scented flowers about the size and something of the shape of the British wild daffodil. Unfortunately, this is rather rare, but after all size is but one quality out of many, and certainly not one essential to beauty or interest. An *Abutilon* is found in dry stream beds.

The existence of perennial, herbaceous vegetation, remaining green after the winter vegetation has shrivelled, in a country where there may be no rain at all for four years[2], a land of scorching sun and hot winds alternating with steamy damp days, where the wells are so salt that ordinary plants die at once when watered from them, where sand-laden gales may cut one's face and grind the surface of glass, is a wonderful display of the power of adaptation to the most adverse conditions, a magnificent success in the struggle for existence. We have the development of a special flora, a selection of plants from many distinct families, which has acquired the ability to live in the salt sands and in crannies of bare rocks by the sea. The commonest of these are two plants which have special beauties. One, *Statice plumbaginoides*, grows generally on bare coral rock, and has large flower-heads of a beautiful pink colour, like sprays of heather contrasting with its dark green leaves. The other, *Suaeda volkensii*, which

---

[1] A species of *Carex* I believe.

[2] I am writing of the neighbourhood of Lat. 22° N. About Suakin conditions are better, at least for plant life.

grows only in sand, has nothing that looks like leaf or flower, but seems to consist of branched rows of translucent green beads. The special beauty of this plant, apart from its shewing green life on such inhospitable sand, is the wonderful tints it takes on at certain times. Every autumn longer spikes appear, which become of brilliant translucent orange or crimson, like the changes of leaves in northern woods. It is a case where the colour is due to the flower bracts, the flowers themselves being inconspicuous.

A few pictures, of summer calm and storm, and my foundations for a visual impression of the country are laid. Just south of Suakin is an area of (approximately) 100 square miles consisting of a labyrinth of coral reefs with winding passages of deep water, and here and there open pools. Slowly my vessel picks its way through the wholly uncharted and unbeaconed maze. There is, indeed, no immediate necessity for aids to navigation, for the breeze, fresh but not strong, ripples the water so that the reefs shew among the blue-green of the deeper channels as clearly as the white squares of a chess board. They are all beautiful shades of green as the water over them is more or less shallow, merging into yellow where a sand-bank approaches the surface, and richest brown where beds of living corals grow. Ahead is the outer reef, an unbroken line of foam separating these calm waters and lighter tints from the deep blue, the colour of a peacock's neck, of the open wave-tossed sea. Landwards are the mountains, faint and hazy in the heat. The coastal plain is invisible under the horizon ; despite our shallow waveless water and the presence of reefs, we are far out at sea.

Two or three native boats, painted dark red, add a finishing touch to the colour scheme. They are anchored in these landless harbours, while their crews are scattered in canoes, mere black specks, searching for the pearl shell oysters which occur here at rare intervals.

My storm picture (see frontispiece) has a similar reef harbour for its foreground, but we are only five miles out at sea on the barrier system, north of Port Sudan. To-day the reefs are barely visible, for with us it is almost a dead calm. All those colours of shoaling sand and coral beds are only visible when the water is rippled. A few stones, mere specks here and there above the glassy surface alone shew the presence of a reef on which no swell is breaking.

Calm is thus more dangerous to a steamer than storm, for should she approach the reef areas before picking up the beacons and lighthouse that mark the entrances to Port Sudan and Suakin, she runs great risk of striking an invisible reef. Sailing vessels are safe, as whenever they are under way the water is rippled and the reefs easily seen.

But landwards peace gives way to storm. The mountains are purple, inky clouds with lurid white edges blot out the blue. The sea is black with wind, white puffs of spindrift rise, drive over the water and disappear again. Some native vessels, which last night may have anchored in land-locked harbours some miles astern of us, are racing before the north wind, only daring to shew a corner of their great lateen main-sails, while we have not wind enough to find our way out of the reef-labyrinth in which we anchored for the night. Later arises a dun-coloured cloud in the north—a dust-storm. Rapidly this bears down upon us, increasing in size as it comes, till it reaches towards the zenith, blotting out the storm clouds, mountains, and plain with a pall as dense as a curtain. For those in the cloud the wind is burning hot[1]; the fine dust covers the face, cakes the eyelashes and even the teeth. One's face is made sore with the impact of the coarser particles; sight is as impossible as in the densest London fog. One must lower one's sails and trust there are no reefs within the distance the vessel may drift before the storm blows itself out. After the dust may come a furious squall of rain.

Here, where rain is so visibly the coming of life to the earth, it is fitly heralded by the full majesty of vast cloud

[1] Actual temperature of the wind 100° to 115° Fahr.

mountains with snowy summits, from whose dark bases issue continuous lightnings and thunder. In such weather heavy squalls may be expected from any quarter, causing much anxiety to sailors used to the regular winds of the Red Sea. One cloud mass may grow until the sky is covered, mountains hidden in a black veil of rain, a furious wind hiding the shore by a great brown cloud of dust. Before the squall reaches the vessel sail is reduced to a mere corner of the great triangle usually spread, amid much excited shouting. Lightning and thunder become almost continuous and the sea is lashed white with rain and spray. It is as cold and dark as night, and impossible to see more than a few yards ahead, all idea of entering harbour is given up and a look-out is kept *downwards* in case the vessel may pass over a shoal (which would be visible five fathoms down, in the clear water) on which she could anchor till the storm passed off. Suddenly a tiny rift appears in the cloud mass ahead ; a mountain top becomes visible through the rain, then the masts of a vessel in harbour. In five minutes we may have passed from darkness, storm, and anxious peering through rain, to the bright sunshine and calm of a summer sea.

Could the love of beauty, the artist's sense of colour, find any object in this bare land, dead yellow rock and sands bordering a waste of sea ? What is there to replace the infinite variety of colour, of ferny rock, heathery moors and sedgy pools of the desert places of our own land ? At times the lover of beauty, even of colour, can be fully satisfied, for the sun alone can throw over this emptiness a glory like that of the golden streets and jewelled gates of the prophet's vision. The sea becomes one splendid turquoise, the coral rock more beautiful than gold, the mountains, mere heaps of dead rock though they are, savage and repellent, change to great tender masses of lovely colour, ruddy violets and pinks, luminous as though they had some source of light within themselves and shared in the joy they give to the solitary beholder; changing as the sun sinks to deeper colder shades, announcing the benediction of a perfect night. Vessels entering harbour, their crews returning home after a week at sea, become fairy craft, each sail like the rare pink pearls found within the rosy edge of certain shells.

To visit sunset land is but a dream of children, happiness is nearer than the sunset clouds. That gold has been thrown about our feet, over the common stones and bitter waters, and we have gathered spiritual wealth. The kingdom of heaven is within us and the vision of Patmos realised.

One thing necessary to the happiness of a nature-lover the desert can never supply. One needs some sight of luxuriant, riotous life, some equivalent for the rapid growth of grass and trees, that overflowing of life that in other lands causes every vacant inch of soil to bear some weed or flower.

The satisfaction of this desire is easily found *in* the Red Sea, not above it. At present the love of the sea gardens is an esoteric pleasure, some day we hope it may become as universal as the love of wild nature inland. Corals to take the place of plants, fishes and lower animals of all kinds, beautiful, bizarre, useful and poisonous, making gardens of teeming life under water, where the very worms are often beautiful as flowers. In the harbours where the water is stagnant, but clearer than any British sea, besides corals are weeds of all kinds and shapes, among which swim numbers of little fish of comical form, quaintly tame and gorgeously coloured. The biologist knows, however, that these strangely coloured weeds, brown, grey, green, violet, red and yellow, are mostly animals like the corals, some are sponges, some, like clusters of brown or grey daisies, a kind of cousin of the coral polyps. That large feathery flower, white, yellow, or reddish brown, will vanish like a flash if touched. It is nothing more nor less than the head of a worm, not much like the slow-moving senseless earthworm, but one which builds a house for its protection among crannies of the stones, into which it can withdraw its plumed head, sensitive to even a passing shadow.

The multitude of forms assumed by the corals, their frequently gorgeous colours, equal anything to be seen in a land garden. These grow in greatest luxuriance outside the harbour where the water is of astonishing clarity. It is owing to the vigour of their growth that the edge of the reef is nearly a vertical wall, so that looking down strange beautiful shapes are seen one below another, weird fish entering and leaving their lairs under the coral tangle, till in the pure blue depths the forms of coral and fish become indistinct and pass into the haze of water 60 feet or more deep.

The portion of the coast I have described is typical of the whole. The mountains may be lower or higher, the plain is narrower in the south, broader in the north, and the sea is varied with a few islands about Rawaya and islets of coral rock or sand form the Suakin Archipelago. These sand cays, if always above highest water-level, are peculiar in bearing quite a dense border of low-growing woody plants, at a level immediately above high tide. The rocky islets are almost entirely bare, yellow in colour, surrounded by cliffs like those described at Shêkh Barûd (Port Sudan), and generally level-topped.

In the thousand miles of this side of the Red Sea coast below Suez there are but two towns, Kossêr, in Egypt, now decayed to a mere village, and Suakin. The new town, Port Sudan, the building of which only began in 1905, is, as the name implies, merely the end of the railway communicating with the real Sudan, "the country of the blacks" far over the mountains, by the Nile. It has no significance as a part of this country; the Briton came, took over the bare desert round the wonderful natural harbour of Shêkh Barûd and built there a perfectly modern town, quay walls that the largest ships may lie alongside, electric cranes for their cargoes, and electric light for the town, a grand opening railway bridge over the harbour and every modern need of a great port and terminus. No longer is the tomb the only mark for sailors; one of the finest lighthouses in the world

stands on Sanganeb Reef, and the harbour itself is complete
with all necessary lights and beacons, the entrance being
naturally as safe and easy as if it had been planned by
Providence as a harbour for big steamers[1].

The Romance of Modern Power did attempt to live with
that of the Eastern beauty of a desert metropolis in old
Suakin, but the site was too cramped and Suakin is now left
much as it was before the railway linked it with the Nile and
made it, for a brief season, a station on a great thoroughfare.

Owing to the existence of the barrier reefs the approach
to Suakin is down a 30-mile passage parallel to the coast, and
from two to five miles wide. The shore becomes very low,
and the fringing-reef wider than near Port Sudan, so that the
distinction between sea and shore would be almost untraceable
but for the presence of those salt-loving plants which grow
everywhere along high water-mark. Suakin is situated
two miles inland, at the head of the inlet which forms its
harbour, yet so low is the land that its houses appear over
the horizon as though standing in the sea. A cluster of tall
houses becomes distinct later over the starboard bow and
finally, when the town is nearly abeam, a channel in the shore

---

[1] Besides the completest possible system of harbour lights, the quays, etc., with
every facility for handling cargo, the needs of shipping are well provided for by a
large stock of coal electrically handled, tugs and water barges, and a complete
dockyard for repairs of any kind up to a considerable magnitude. Since 1910 a
salvage tug has been stationed here and the slipway at the dockyard has been
completed and is in use. The town water supply, though healthy, is slightly brackish
(though much less so than most desert wells), but the very large condensing plants
produce and sell fresh water very cheaply. The railway of course runs alongside
the shipping, the Customs godowns are liberally and conveniently planned, and
the railway bridge rises vertically upwards so that any vessel may pass up to the
dockyard without obstruction.

A first-class hotel has just been opened.

Spite of the harbour's being practically tideless its water is perfectly pure, all
garbage being collected in barges and towed out to sea, where they are emptied at
a distance of about five miles from land.

The whole town is a fine example of what can be done by scientific forethought
given free scope and a clear desert site, unhampered by the presence of partially
obsolete arrangements and conflicting vested interests, and keeping ever in view
the great extensions of every department which the increasing trade of the Sudan
will soon need.

reef, hitherto invisible, opens out and, instead of a harbour we enter a narrow winding natural canal of deep water, passing

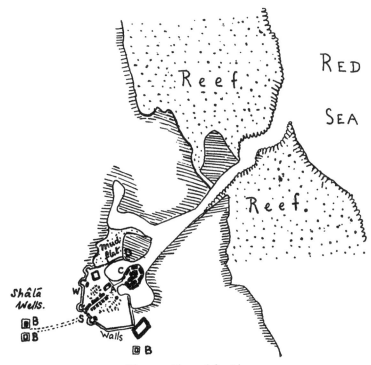

Fig. 4. Plan of Suakin

for a mile through the shallow water on the reefs, its course marked by the contrast between its deep blue and the varying pearly tints of the reef shallows. The regularity of the canal

Fig. 5. SUAKIN. The Customs House and Government buildings (C on plan)

is astonishing when one remembers that it is purely natural, and not a river but an inlet of the sea. Then the reefs are replaced by low-lying land of yellow coral rock. We pass the tombs of shêkhs, cubical or domed, each with its set of tattered flags which are presented at intervals by the pious. Before us the harbour expands slightly and the canal forks; an island thus formed bears a solid mass of tall and graceful white houses, beneath which, to the right, cluster the short sloping masts of native vessels; beyond all, over the sunlit plain, the mountains. I know no other town which can compare with Suakin in the fair white dignity which it shews to one approaching. It is the realisation of one's romantic image of an Arabian desert town. No higher praise could be given than by saying that this fair view of Suakin may replace and enlarge the image of our romantic dreams, and yet I give this praise deliberately, careless of contradiction.

Suakin is indeed a long way from being a city of palaces, as its residents know full well. There are no cathedral mosques, no citadel like that of Cairo. The buildings which made our view of fairyland include quite prosaic offices of the Bank, Quarantine, Eastern Telegraph, the Government House and the Customs. The rest are private houses occupied by very ordinary persons, Arab merchants and so on. All are either Arab buildings slightly adapted to their modern uses, or built by Arab architects in their own style. I suppose Suakin owes its fascination largely to its site. The houses appear so high and graceful, rising as they do directly from the water's edge or from land only a foot or two above that level. Then the two branches of the harbour enclose it and render its boundary definite and compact, no straggling into dingy suburbs, on this side at least, and yet no hiding of the true town behind walls. Frankly, complete and self-contained, calmly the town faces the never-ruffled waters of its harbour, and looks over the great plain towards mountains and sea. Jedda, by comparison, is a finer and larger town, with more of architectural beauty, and also purely Arabian, but it is on the open shore, so lacking the ordered approach, the definiteness of site of Suakin, lying in its arms of the sea.

Plate *IV*

Fig. 6. A Suakin Mosque
(*Photo by W. H. Lake, Esq.*)

We do not expect much noise of traffic in the city of our fairyland, nor much display in the public buildings of our desert city. True this ancient and religious city is full of white-washed mosques, and of domes over the tombs of shêkhs, but their minarets are often no higher than the surrounding houses, and marble pillars give place to painted wood, but the minarets, short and free from carving and other ornament though they be, are quaintly graceful; they are neither Turkish nor Egyptian, but purely Arabian in design (Plate IV)[1]. One would not wish to alter the stern yet peace-giving simplicity of the places where generations of men of the desert and sea have prayed, for the more ornate buildings of richer lands.

Well do I remember waking at sunrise after a night spent under the stars on a flat house-roof, to a scene of beauty that does much to reconcile me to the monotony and loneliness of exile in Suakin, and help me to bear the terrible heat of summer days. Sunrise over the sea, a great blaze of gold following the pearly pinks which made the sky like the inside of a lovely shell. Houses and mosques purest white, no stain shewing in that fresh light. Over the grey plain I cannot tell whether what I see is mere gravel or a layer of grey morning mist, from which rise the deep red foot-hills, and beyond are the high mountains in perfect clearness, first purple then ruddy, all detail visible, yet with no loss of aerial perspective. From the harbour below come the voices of sailors, "Al-lah, Al-lah" is the word distinct among the babel as they call upon God and His Prophet for help in the task in hand. But one who has come in from a sojourn of weeks in the desert rests his eye with infinite pleasure on a spot in the near distance, the oasis of Shâta, where, just beyond the embankment between two of the forts which were built to keep Suakin from the dervishes, the tops of green trees nestle. One promises oneself a walk out there to the trees and

---

[1] Many of the smaller mosques in Egypt, particularly those near the deserts (e.g. Suez and Belbês) are very similar.

gardens in the afternoon, when it is not cool indeed, but still a little cooler. Meanwhile though the sun has risen not half an hour it is scorching already, and one must seek shelter from it and prepare for the day's work.

A history of Suakin would be worth reading, but it remains mostly unwritten ; though since the times of Gordon it might be extracted from reports and newspapers. Gordon was once Governor-General of the Red Sea, and the " Mudiria," or Government House of Suakin, was his official headquarters. Traces of the railway begun for his relief in Khartûm, but never finished, the outlying forts once attacked by dervish fanatics, are within easy reach, and the nearer ones for the defence of the Shâta Wells and the town itself are close at hand. Even the rifle trenches, the barbed wire entanglements and such temporary defences, though nothing has been done for their preservation, are still present to shew how near, in Suakin, we are to those famous fights.

Plate V

Fig. 7. Suakin. The causeway and town gate (A on plan)

Fig. 8. Suakin. One of Kitchener's forts (B on plan)

Fig. 9. Sunset on the Red Sea

Plate VI

Fig. 10. A young man of the Amarar
(*Note absence of sewn clothing*)

CHAPTER II

SOCIAL AND RELIGIOUS CONDITIONS

NOTE. My account of the natives is based on my dealings with the people at a point about a hundred miles north of Port Sudan, on the boundary between the tribes of Bisharia and Amarar, but it would apply to those of the south in most essentials.

Nationalities

THREE perfectly distinct nationalities have representatives on this coast[1]. Besides the natives proper there are true Arabs from the other side of the Red Sea, and negroes, who are slaves or the descendants of slaves brought over the mountains from the upper Nile valley.

The true natives are called, and call themselves, Arabs, and many of them speak Arabic. For all that they are no more Arabs than they are Europeans, being of Hamitic not of Semitic race, allied to the ancient Egyptians and far less

---

[1] The population of my own tiny village well illustrates the cosmopolitan nature of all commercial and administrative activity in the Sudan ; including Government *employés* we have :

British : one, myself.

Syrians : two, my assistant and a carpenter.

Italian : one, engineer—we communicate in Arabic.

Egyptians : about six.

Arabians : also about six, including natives of Sinai in the north and the Yemen and Hadramaut in the south.

Hamites : the natives of the country.

Negroes : these include several distinct nationalities, e.g. Nubas and Nilotic tribes.

Swahili : one, from Zanzibar.

Elsewhere Greeks abound, as in so many countries.

We all speak Arabic, which was however the mother tongue of only a dozen individuals, and even these speak three or four different dialects !

mingled with Arab blood than are the so-called "Arabs" of
Modern Egypt[1].

This western shore being altogether too poor a country
for the evolution of real sea-going vessels, and the Arabs of
the eastern side being one of the first of the sailor and exploring
nations of the world, it is no wonder that all the traffic of the
Red Sea is carried out by Arabs, and that Arabs are to be
found in every village of the coast.   Besides the sailors they
supply the shop-keepers, merchants and skilled artisans, and
nowadays many come over to work as labourers in Port
Sudan.   The two types, Hamitic natives and Semitic Arabs,
can therefore be seen together and contrasted very easily.
(Compare Figs. 11, 12 and 13 on Plate VII and Fig. 10.)
Apart from dress the following important physical differences
are obvious at first sight.   The West Coast man is generally
the taller, much darker in colour, and with smaller features,
especially a smaller and straighter nose.   He is as often
"good looking" as is the Arab, and that perhaps, is the
most generally appreciable difference between him and the
negro.   In contrast with the Arab his hair is a "fuzzy" mop
not *jet* black[2] nor merely curly.   His beard[3] is scantier,
though to both it is the most precious of personal beauties.
Mentally, though many are very intelligent, he is the inferior
of the Arab who has occupied all the skilled trades in the
country, but he is the superior again of the negro.   It is
however debateable whether this effect may not be partly due
to the civilisation of a more populous and richer country
having brought out the capabilities of those Arabs who
possess any.

[1] I am at a loss for a name for this particular Hamitic nation.   The names
Hadendoa, Bisharia and so on, are those of large tribal subdivisions of one nation-
ality, which again is but one out of several distinct Hamitic peoples.   The name
"Beja" is not known to any native I have met.

[2] Apart from the use of henna, I have detected a distinct red tinge in some
men's hair, but the wonderful gold and brown mops of the Somalis are not
seen here.

[3] Some Arabs grow bushy beards as dense as any European's, but the majority,
at any rate before middle age have only scanty beards, if any.

Plate VII

Fig. 11. An Arabian Sea captain

Fig. 12. An old man of the Bisharin

Fig. 13. A negro ex-slave

I have had closer personal acquaintance, than is generally possible to an Englishman, with more than fifty natives, and know the character and capabilities of each individual among them. Some are intelligent, some stupid, varying extremely, just as much as a corresponding number of English labourers. On the whole I should think too that they vary between much the same limits. Our chief sailor, an Arab, is not far ahead of the best of the natives, and Arabs I have met are often as stupid as the less intelligent of the latter.

The negroes are quite distinct. To begin with they are black, not merely chocolate brown, with a blackness that hardly admits of shades, and differ from the other races in all the well-known negro characteristics, such as shape of nose and lips, poor development of calf, and the curious way the hair grows in little patches.

We thus have every possible shade of colour between yellow and densest black. The Arab merchant or teacher, who rarely exposes himself to the sun, is hardly dark enough to be called brown, but his poorer brethren become darker, those who labour much in the sun being as dark as the lighter Hamites. These vary down to the darkest chocolate, and then we have the negroes. I well remember my introduction to three new sailors who had been engaged for me in Port Sudan. There appeared a huge negro, coal black, a giant with a gentle voice, and on either side of him a little yellow Arab, like two canary birds hand in hand with a crow.

Socially, the negroes come lowest in the scale; even if slaves no longer, they are treated as complete outsiders in all affairs, and in general with a kindly contempt. I notice for instance that when the villagers go fishing two by two in their canoes negroes pair off together, never Hamite and negro in one canoe. At the same time the headman of a larger sailing vessel always wishes to include a few negroes in his crew, their honesty and tractability, combined with great strength, being qualities which counterbalance dislike to close contact with them in a cramped space.

Intermarriage between Hamite and negro must be rare, as I have met no case[1]. If the village contains no negro women, the male negro must remain unmarried, and no regular marriage between a Hamite man and a black woman has come under my observation, though this union is the more likely to occur. Exceptional men from among them have always risen at intervals, and the British rule, in giving a greater equality of opportunity to all races, will cause more negroes to come to the front. There is some intermingling between the two first races, as Arab sailors are not different from others in liking to have a wife in every port, but it is not at all extensive. The Arabs form no permanent settlement on the coast, the sailor classes at least rarely or never bringing over their women, and the merchants save money to end their days at home. Labourers and sailors will only contract for limited periods ; they are soon homesick and go off with their savings for so long as the latter will last. Of the Arabs in my employ only one has settled down and taken a wife on this side. While the native sailor is always in debt and scarcely able to live on his wages (whether £2 a month or £3, it is all the same in many cases) I was astonished at one Arab who kept coming to me and handing over money for safe keeping until I had £5 or so besides what other savings he had. Having accumulated this fortune he gave me a month's notice and went off to his own country, returning and saving when that was spent. One of my men who was getting the magnificent wages of £4 a month brought his old father-in-law over, but the suggestion that he should also bring his wife and settle down in the house I promised to build for him was met simply by the regretful statement, " It is not our custom to bring our women over the sea." He has so lost the best job he is likely to find in the Red Sea, for soon after he declared he could no longer stand being away from his own people and returned home.

---

[1] Contrast Zanzibar and the tropical coast of East Africa where nearly the whole population is supposed to be a cross between Arab and negro.

In my village at least there is a strong prejudice against such marriages, and the above is the reason. Among less than a hundred families I know of two cases where a daughter has married an Arab and been left with a young family to support, with her father's and brothers' assistance. Naturally that makes the Arab distinctly unpopular as a son-in-law.

The negroes, being a minority and, though permanent residents, not natives of the country, I have less to say of them and so dispose of them first.

I have already referred to their comparatively industrious and frugal habits, and to their subordination. These qualities are less romantic than are the desert restlessness and blood feuds of the Hamites, but they endear them to the administrator, whether of justice or of work.

In manner some are undignified, just "jolly niggers," but others have as good a bearing as any Arab.

They have all been slaves, some to within a year or two, their histories demonstrating the efficacy of the government's repression of slave dealing, even within the country, and in the second and third of the cases I give, the proof is striking.

Several have very similar stories. They remember little of their capture, in remote provinces of the Sudan, as all were then boys of ten or twelve at most. One remembers that his father was killed. Four practically began life in Jedda, where they were first set to tend camels, then sent with the pearling fleet up and down the coast, even as far as Aden and Jibûti, in French Somaliland. At this time several formed friendships which induced them to foregather in my village when they were free.

After years in the pearling fleet, three were sold in Suakin to "Arabs" of the Atbara district, many miles inland, over the mountains and desert, towards Berber. A fourth reached the same tribe by a more adventurous way. Peacefully tending camels for his master near Handûb, in the Red Sea hills, in ignorance of the vicinity of war, he suddenly found himself in the midst of battle[1], and, after receiving a stray bullet through the leg, was carried off by Osman Digna's dervishes in their flight to Tokar.

After the capture of Tokar in 1891, this being the conclusion of the war on the Red Sea coast, he was sold to pearlers from Masawa, finally, at Suakin, to the tribe from the Atbara.

Two others, who had been born in the service of one master in the above-mentioned district, are here. One explained his presence, across hundreds of miles of desert and the Red Sea mountains, by stating that he had heard that his "brother" was doing well in Suakin. There was no romantic desert flight, he took the train near Berber, with his master's concurrence, possibly with his assistance also. His owner had said simply, "I have all the slaves I can manage, go or stay as you like." Such a permission, given freely to two slaves of the most valuable kind, about thirty years old, of powerful physique, intelligent, docile and industrious, is emphatic evidence of the impossibility of sale nowadays. If a secret sale could have been effected, the sacrifice would have been too great, even for an old man anxious to lay up treasure in Heaven.

It is strange enough to find in this tiny village on the edge of the world, men from Darfur and the sources of the Nile, but we have even a Swahili from Zanzibar. Old Mabrûk's life has been far from that of the "Blessed One" his name signifies. He was kidnapped when a boy of ten or twelve, in the days of old Sultan Bargash, away from the island of plenty, to spend the rest of his days on desert coasts. The old ruse, of offering him some coppers to carry a parcel aboard a *sambûk*, started him on the journey from which he never returned. He found himself with "two hundred" others beating up desert coasts for "seven months[2]," through

---

[1] Presumably General Grenfell's engagement with the dervishes, Dec. 1888.

[2] Inverted commas indicate quotations from Mabrûk's statement. The probability is that the hardships of a seven months' voyage were actually compressed into so many weeks.

Plate VIII

Fig. 14. Old Mabrûk, from Zanzibar

Fig. 15. Hamitic woman
Two cotton shawls form her complete
dress

the Gate of Tears into the Red Sea, to Hodêda, and thence to Jedda. There they were thrust into a tiny house by the sea (here Mabrûk indicated my bookshelf as approximately the size of the house!) and sold a few at a time at night.

After a year in Jedda he was sent in a *sambûk* loaded with camels to Suakin, where he obtained his liberty, he scarcely knows how. He was employed aboard a *sambûk* used by Government to convey money and stores to its *employés* at the three coast villages, and in the course of time his son was with him as his fellow-sailor. One night, while in fancied security in a desert harbour, they were set upon by "forty" Arabians, who took them, the Government money, stores, and all, to Jedda. Here he was a slave again, working at collecting fodder in a state of semi-starvation. Two others of the crew had escaped in the night; the rest, including his son, were taken inland and he never saw them again. His skipper, being a freeman, a Hamite not a negro, was not enslaved, but was an exile, until an acquaintance from this side found him and took him home to Suakin. The portrait of this veteran is shewn on Plate X.

After three months came his great adventure, his crossing the whole Red Sea in a stolen canoe, a mere dug-out about fifteen feet long by a little over two broad. This feat is part of one of the stories of Saint Flea (page 37) and seemed legendary until Mabrûk appeared, a man who had done it in actual life, and whose canoe is in sight from my window.

Like the saint· he had no store of food and but little water; it was dead calm, and only those who have been exposed to the Red Sea sun can appreciate the wonder of his endurance, in paddling for eight days, and of his good fortune in landing at the only village in three hundred miles of coast. The present Governor of the Red Sea Province, being on a tour of inspection, revived the half dead man with wine, food, and water, and sent him on to Suakin, where the "Pasha" gave him three months' pay and offered him work on another *sambûk*. He was tired of the sea, and preferred to wander up the coast in his stolen canoe, gaining a precarious living by fishing.

The old man's misfortunes have left him some humour yet, he chuckles delightedly at the idea of his secure and honourable possession of the stolen canoe, forgetting the suffering with which he paid for it, and how near he was to death by thirst, or more mercifully, by the waves of the sea.

Another, who was skipper of a coasting vessel until he went blind lately, and whose portrait is on Plate VII, was stolen in Kordofan when a boy, and taken to Cairo, where shopping with the cook is all the hard labour he remembers. Then his master, in pious mood, gave him his paper of freedom, "for the sake of our Lord." This happened at Suez, which led the freedman to the life on merchant and pearling *sambûks* which he has followed since, and which has thrice taken him as far as Basra on the Euphrates.

It was at Aden he heard that money was to be had in vast quantities by labourers, in the making of the new town of Port Sudan, and there he was engaged for me as ordinary sailor by the Arabian skipper of my little schooner, who once had been his cabin boy or midshipman, or whatever the equivalent may be aboard a *sambûk*!

From what I gather, this is the first time he has spent more than a year in one place, or had a hut he could call his own, though his beard is going grey.

After a few years' service in my vessels he went blind, and is reduced to living on charity, for once well deserved. Even this was not his only trouble, for the Hamites wished to take away his baby son, to be brought up as a slave, denying his paternity. This may, we hope, be prevented.

Having placed our man among the other nationalities in the country, we want to know what he is like to meet and to deal with, how he spends his time and gets his living, what he thinks about, and how this reacts upon his actions, in short, what kind of a man he is.

Plate IX

Fig. 16. An elderly Bishari

I may say at once, that my experience has quite shaken my belief (if I ever held it) in the usual notion that :

"East is East, and West is West, and never the twain shall meet."

The great mysteries of the East are the mysteries of all humanity, and as you may scratch the Russian and find a Tartar, so you may scratch an " Eastern " and find,—just a man, much like the rest of us.

When we meet our friend we generally see a tall, well-made man, light in build but strong and active, often good-looking, with a pleasant and self-respecting expression. He may rise as we pass, to shew respect, but offers no salutation unless his superior should salute first. If we speak to him he will address us respectfully, yet as an equal, first shaking hands as he would to one of his own nation. If he is not a very poor man, or engaged in manual labour, he is probably much more gracefully dressed than we are, in the folds of yards of calico looped about his person, leaving arms and neck free. True his hair, a great fuzzy mop, plastered with mutton fat, looks a trifle ridiculous and even unclean, but Burton e.g. has, after experience, much to say in favour of a free use of grease in a tropical climate. Or he may wear a turban, which appears more dignified to European eyes, being more familiar.

He displays his freedom, his membership of a desert community, not only by his self-reliant look, but by his always carrying arms. As we meet him, his camel has been tethered[1] before the shop where he is obtaining provisions, and his sword, shield, or spear given into the merchant's keeping, our mountaineer retaining only a dagger, stuck into a loose heavy leather belt, or having its sheath bound round his arm, just above the elbow. The former dagger is generally a curved blade nine inches or so long, the latter a small broad

---

[1] The camel kneels and his halter rope is bound round one foreknee. Only a fractious beast will rise when so tied, and straying or running away is impossible.

dagger with a plain round handle. The sheaths are very ornamental, bearing embossed patterns and strips of green leather among the brown.

Neither is he anything but proud of the evidences of his religion and superstitions. There may be a circular patch of dust in the middle of his forehead, where he touched the ground, bowing in prayer, and his amulets, paper charms wrapped up in little square leather cases worn as a necklace, or, more often, tied round the arm immediately above the elbow, and his string of prayer beads, are his principal ornaments. He may wear a ring or two, on his fingers, and a narrow band round his arm, both of silver, while a thin curved skewer, of hard wood or ibex horn, thrust through his hair, completes his adornment.

In conversation we find him generally intelligent, rarely surly or ill-behaved. Having self-respect himself he appreciates and returns politeness, and is not so foolish as to interpret it as weakness. In travelling through the desert any dusty old man will expect you to give a friendly greeting, and the news, and smile upon you as a friend. Unfortunately the language is rather a stumbling-block, as many natives are not fluent in Arabic, and few British know the Hamitic speech. However, for a friendly salutation Arabic (or perhaps any language!) will suffice anywhere.

An introduction to a woman is not so easily arranged. Though the women are only partially secluded, and are not veiled, even if one knows the husband, sons, and brothers of a family quite well, the women shew a distinct reserve. One knows their character largely through complaints brought by their husbands, for not only does the British lord of a desert village become their father in name, but he is dragged at intervals into the consideration of intimate family concerns. Also in no country can "Cherchez la femme" be a better motto for investigating any dispute. They appear in the background of every lawsuit and complaint, even if it at first seems to concern men alone, and when men would let a doubtful

.

Plate X

Fig. 17. A veteran seaman

Fig. 18. Hair dressed with mutton fat weeks ago

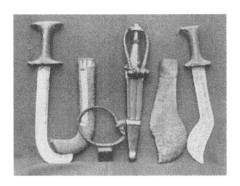

Fig. 19. Three daggers and an amulet

Fig. 20. Woman's hand with stalked rings, etc.

claim go by, it is the women who insist on their rights, as keenly on fancied as on real, and send their men before the magistrate.

In person they are rather slight, and well made like the men. In accordance with their more sheltered life they are lighter in colour, and their dress and ornaments are altogether different, for instance the hair is plaited into a number of tight little tails, and the fat which is rubbed in is mixed with soot. It is nearly long enough to reach their shoulders, and is decorated with strings of beads and thin plates of gold. Sometimes these are in quite good taste, in other cases the effect is merely barbaric. Though the men dress in white only (a white which speedily becomes the general tint of the desert), the women practically always wear coloured cotton stuff. Dark blue with a red and yellow border is common, but the fashion now in my village is for a red stuff with yellow threads interwoven. Two pieces make the complete outfit, one being tied round the waist reaches the feet, the other is laid shawl fashion about the shoulders, and, in the case of married women, over the head as well. The women are not veiled, but on meeting a white man they generally draw part of their garment over their mouths.

Their ornaments consist of strings of beads round neck and waist, silver rings for fingers and ankles, and, if possible, gold (or gilt) ornaments for nose and ears.

I give illustrations of some of the ornaments on Plate X ; note the curious ring, stalked to display its stone, which may be mere coloured glass or such a stone as cornelian. The nose ring must be a trying discomfort. It is often my fate to administer medicine, and, before drinking, the nose ring must be pushed aside, and held so, I suppose, whenever anything is put to the mouth. The ankles bear large scars made by the friction of the rings when they were first worn.

They are just as good-looking and intelligent as their husbands, and young women and girls are often very pretty, the former in spite of their nose rings. But the circumstances of their lives often give the older women a hard expression, though I know of old women living in the most abject poverty who remain models of genial good-nature.

The fact that the northern[1] and southern tribes, otherwise of similar customs and beliefs, differ altogether in such a fundamental matter as female morality, is instructive. In the south a girl who became pregnant illegitimately would run a great risk of death at the hands of her relatives, in the north it would be easily condoned. Not only so, but a woman is the more valued by her husband if she gives proof of her attractiveness to other men, even by adultery; he has no resentment against his wife, his honour being satisfied by an attack with his dagger on the first meeting with his rival.

The explanation that suggests itself is that the lesser rainfall of the north, making the country able to support but a sparse population, necessitates a greater restriction of the natural increase than in the more habitable south. In the northern deserts war is unknown, pestilence cannot flame from end to end of so scattered a people, and local famines can be more or less avoided by nomads, the men of whom are so inured to hard fare as to be able to travel for days on dry uncooked "dûra" corn alone. Hence the postponement of marriage which, combined with oriental licence, brings about the result with equal certainty, and greater misery, than do that awful trinity, War, Pestilence, and Famine.

The women may easily excuse themselves to the western critic by asking why they should be faithful to a contract in the making of which they had no voice, and sexual immorality cannot here be condemned as a sin against the race as it is in the West.

In spite of the use of weapons, in private or in tribal quarrels, examples of which I describe later, I consider no

---

[1] I am told that the sexual freedom of women is a peculiarity of one tribe only —the Aliab—but it certainly applies to all the maritime people with whom I live.

really lawless or unintelligent race could have built up, and maintained, the administration they have, under the circumstances of desert life. They are elaborately subdivided into tribes and family groups under Shêkhs[1], of superior and subordinate ranks, whose decisions they respect as a rule. The Government has found the system workable, and on the whole confines its attention to perfecting and supplementing it where necessary. Cases brought before a magistrate are often, after hearing, referred back to a Shêkh, whose decision is, if necessary, backed up by the Civil Power. No Englishman need carry any arms in living in or passing through their country, and, at least in the north, he need have no fear of theft. They are perfectly contented with the Government and respect all its agents, pay their taxes and obey the decisions of either magistrates or their own Shêkhs. They have a lively recollection of the Mahdist General, Osman Digna, and their gratitude for, and jubilation over his downfall is still expressed in ordinary conversation. I had polite enquiries for him the other day, with remarks on the impoverishment of the country which he caused. I fear my sailor was disappointed to hear that he was not yet dead. Osman Digna's men, "fuzzies" though they were, were either foreigners brought into the country and living upon its already poor inhabitants, or conscripts taken more or less by force. In any case there was very little fighting so far north as my station.

Arms, though but rarely used, are regarded as indispensable, and no native goes a mile or two away from the towns unarmed. A leather belt, generally a very broad heavy affair, ornamented with patterns cut into it, carries the typical

---

[1] The word Shêkh, meaning literally an old man, is used to designate alike a dead saint of the highest supernatural powers or one whose sanctity is barely acknowledged by an occasional decoration of his tomb by a piece of rag on a stick. Among the living the Shêkh may be a native leader of any grade, from the head of a great tribe, with whom the British Governor of a Province may consult, and to whom is entrusted real power, to one of his subordinate agents. In my village one of these combines the trade of butcher with a dreadful dentistry.

curved knife or "khangar[1]"; or a straight dagger may be carried in a sheath which is tied round the arm immediately above the elbow. One of these together with a very hard heavy stick, slightly curved, and not used as a walking-stick, is the ordinary man's equipment, but if he goes on a journey he takes as well a round leather shield and long sword or a spear. If afoot he carries the former on his back, the sword under his arm like an umbrella. Perhaps the fact that he does not carry them after the style of the hero of romance only emphasises the fact that they are carried as a matter of sober business. The wounds that I have dealt with have been mere flesh wounds and apparently had been inflicted with the curved khangar, which seems beautifully adapted to give showy wounds without going so deep as to endanger life. In two cases, the jugular or carotid had been aimed at, but missed, though the great angular gash resulting was a sufficiently disgusting sight. Almost all the natives one meets have great scars and the reasons they give for them are generally "only a little talk," but of course women are concerned with most. Trivial private quarrels have a way of becoming inter-tribal in our neighbourhood, as we are on the boundary between the Bisharia and Amarar. For instance two of the more serious cases which have come about during my residence here arose as follows :

A man drawing water for his camels fell into the well and another laughed at him. Unfortunately the two men were of different tribes and a fight resulted, one man was knocked senseless by a blow given end-on by one of their thick and heavy sticks, and two more were badly cut about with knives. The former was expected to die at any moment, and his death would confer on his relatives the right and duty of killing the murderer, or, failing him, his next of kin. They declared their intention, as soon as the man should die, of coming for two of my *employés*, who were related to the murderer but who had been at work with me during the fight,

---

[1] Anglicised into "hangar."

Plate XI

Fig. 21. Our postman, starting for his hundred mile ride, armed
with sword and shield

so I was appealed to. I proposed to send the threatened men
away by boat, but to pass the reefs by night was a difficulty.
All the head boat men declared it impossible and declined the
risk except one, the younger and more adventurous, who took
them through and has gloried in the feat since.

There was some danger of a general fight between the
two tribes, but a third and impartial set came down from the
hills to keep the peace. Next day came requests that we
should dress the wounds. So, my wife accompanying me, we
rode out to a tent among the trees, in the dark depths of
which we found two savage half-witted looking men stolidly
sitting sniffing onion and spices with which their noses were
plugged to prevent them inhaling any possible odour of their
wounds. Each had three or four cuts about six or eight
inches long and one to two deep. I tried more or less to
close up the edges of the cuts in one man's back, which would
have caused great pain to a white man ; if I hurt this one at
all he only shewed it by laughing. We were far from laughter
in that dark and smelling tent and glad to get under way
again. We were then led to the house of the dying man and
found a tent among the acacia bushes surrounded by a semicircle of men sitting silently to await what might befall, every
man fully armed with swords, daggers and spears, apparently
ready to wreak vengeance the moment the victim should die.
We found the man sitting in the middle of the tent, a roughly
circular hole in his forehead exposing the pulsating brain.
We could do nothing for him ; it would have been no use
suggesting sending him to Port Sudan hospital, though that
might have saved his life. Of course the man was completely
unconscious, his sitting up was explained by the fact that he
remained in any position in which he might be placed. It
was more than a week before he died and meanwhile the
murderer had gone into the country of another tribe. For
the present he is safe, but should he return without the blood
money his life is forfeit. It is usual for a murderer to collect
say £10 from the charitable, the payment of which to the

next of kin to the murdered man may be the condition of peace between them. One imagines him on his tramp repeating, "I am a poor man and having committed a murder, a most worthy object of your charity. Give me a little towards the blood money." It seems an easy way of settling for a murder, but five to ten years' exile as a beggar in another tribe must be a very serious thing for these family-loving people. It is at any rate less barbarous than that horror of civilisation, penal servitude for life. It is one of those cases where the ends of justice are well served by the Government's policy of leaving, under supervision, whatever of administration can justly be left to the natural rulers of these wanderers among inaccessible mountains.

In this particular case I hear the avengers are implacable, no mediation will induce them to accept blood money, they must have the murderer's life.

Another quarrel arose from a debt of one shilling only, the debtor refusing to pay. The creditor came to complain to me when I was busy in my office and I put him off awhile. He came again and said something about somebody striking him. I said I would see about it directly. Five minutes later on going out I found four men sitting on the sand each in a little pool of blood, and a crowd waving sticks coming up from the village. The first thing was to meet the crowd and make my men take possession of all the sticks and knives and throw them into my store, but such was the excitement that some would part with their stick to no one but myself. This done I spent two hours bandaging the wounds of those four men. I suppose there would be sixteen cuts altogether. None made the smallest sign of pain. One, a boy of about eighteen, who had lost a good deal of blood through the severing of a vein, looked rather sleepy. We hope soon to be too civilised for these scenes and nowadays the carrying of knives in the village, except in the case of men actually coming in from or starting out upon a journey, is being punished by the confiscation of the knife, and fighting otherwise discouraged.

Just as their system of Government is patriarchal, so also the junior members of their community treat each other with a consideration and good nature one would be glad to see more of, among blood-brothers in other lands. They work together with invariable good humour, an extra man never shirking his share of work, but often insisting that his turn at the oar, e.g., is due before his fellow is willing to give it up. Heavy labour is accompanied by song and invocations of God and the Prophet, and work in a big, noisy crowd, is one of the pleasures of life. I remember once when timber was being unloaded from a *sambûk*, work continued after hours, but a suitable song being started, and extra men being put on, turned the whole thing into a game; as each man threw down his load he dashed back along the pier at a dancing run, to receive another plank with the eagerness a child shews over sweets. There is nothing very inspiriting in the songs as a rule, mere vain repetitions such as :

Recit. "Moses stood at the door."
Chorus. "At the door."

Who Moses was I have not discovered, except that it is *not* the prophet but another of that name.

In Unison. "The night comes,
The night comes,"

was sung at about six o'clock in the morning!

This makes them extremely pleasant to work with, and though among a number of *employés* disputes necessarily occur, and slackness has to be rebuked, I do not feel that I should get more work from members of a "superior" race, and I doubt whether I should be able to be on the same friendly footing with them. In intelligence they vary widely, just as do members of any other nationality or any class, and while some are only at the level of European labourers and factory hands, others could be trained to become good rough carpenters and blacksmiths, while a man capable of managing a boat well, through all the chances and intricacies of a ten days' voyage, and able to preserve discipline among his crew, shews skill and intelligence of no mean order.

From what has been said so far, one would imagine social conditions to be almost Utopian, but just as the Mohammedan religion is admirable from one aspect, and a degradation from another, so the patriarchal system, which breeds self-reliance with subordination, tribal patriotism and consideration for fellows, also produces a strength of public opinion, which, coupled with the absence of privacy inseparable from life in small communities of overcrowded and unfenced tents, becomes a grinding ever present tyranny. The action of any more clear-sighted man who should arise among them would thus be instantly and automatically extinguished, superstition is stereotyped, a man's life is hedged in with restrictions, which are absurd because the meanings they have had are now utterly forgotten[1]. There is nothing more unfortunate than the great idea many British express, of the wonderful knowledge the "Arabs" possess, which is held to transcend all that mere western methods can ever discover. Put to the test, by a careful examination of the working of their own particular interests, say camel breeding and pearl fishing, this wonderful science all falls down to rule of thumb, coupled with that sublime assurance in making unfounded assertions which is the prerogative of the very ignorant. A year or two's acquaintance with either industry will put a careful observer into possession of more knowledge than has been accumulated from hoary ages of rule of thumb and the lazy theorising which is the parent of all superstition.

Again, the fearful loss caused by the absence of love, with its concomitant immorality and suffering, is largely due to the levelling *down* which results from the tyranny of public opinion. The partnership of man and woman which, in our

---

[1] I give a few examples, but Dr and Mrs Seligmann, being expert anthropologists, were able to extract more curious information from my own men in half an hour's talk than I had done in five years. Their report will be of the highest interest.

ideal, is closer than any other, is impossible under their conditions of life, which make privacy and individuality so difficult, and men are not the more eager to marry, where that involves coming even further under the fetters of custom, and the giving of all the wife's relatives, as well as those of blood, a voice in their private affairs.

One symptom of this state of things is the fact that a married woman is often more loyal to her brothers than to her husband, and it is a common complaint that she is supporting able-bodied brothers in idleness, on her husband's earnings, without his leave and, so far as possible, without his knowledge.

I believe that in this all powerful patriarchal rule we touch upon a cause of much of the difference, for good or evil, between East and West, the stagnation of the East generally as well as the all powerful solidarity of Japan.

Of the Mohammedan religion the same may be said. It is attractive to most of those who approach it with any sympathy, to whom a religion for *men*, the ideal of proud yet ready submission to Almighty God, set forth by a ritual hardly surpassed in dignity by any, must appeal strongly. Yet here again is the tyranny of dead customs, the awful, blinding influence of Bibliolatry. Everything that was knowable was spoken to the Prophet by the messenger of God Himself, and to add to, or subtract from that knowledge, is sin. The customs and ideas of a provincial town, in the middle of desert Arabia, thus become unalterable laws for all the world, and those who will not acknowledge this are infidels, damned to the wrath of God.

In this atmosphere all advance in knowledge, all testing of theories by experiment, is mere foolishness, and though the infidel, whom the mysterious will of God has placed over them, may be their Friend and Father when all is well, let but some trifling incident pit his knowledge against theirs, and he will find that he is no longer the light shining in a dark place that he fondly imagined, but a mere ignorant meddler in matters that are too high for him; his poor "savage" children are the elect, the possessors of light and infallible guidance, he is in the darkness, groping among the beggarly elements, and occupying himself with ridiculous trifles. Very annoying indeed, and very trying to the temper of His Excellency, the British Magistrate, is it to have this fact rubbed in by personal experience, but it has a fine educative value. Even when he comes home, and studies the social problems of Britain, he will soon meet and be thwarted by members of his own nation who have all the essential characteristics of the typical Eastern, though clothed in different ideas, and will find that East and West not only meet, but inextricably intermingle.

In theory the often ridiculous miracle stories of Mohammedanism are non-essentials, in practice they impress the average believer far more than do the high religious moral ideals which are set forth with, and by, them. We must guard against thinking that our dark friends' morality and actions are much influenced by his formal religion, it is only the general tendency, falling in as it does with his social ideas, which has any influence.

CHAPTER III

RELIGIOUS OBSERVANCES AND SUPERSTITIONS

THE forms of religion are inextricably interwoven with every event of the people's lives. As the sailors pull at a heavy rope there are cries upon God and the Prophet for help, and as the rope begins to give to the strain, the long-drawn " Pray," " Pray," " Oh, God, Oh Prophet " gives place to a quicker chant, " God gives it, God gives it." To the enquiry "Are you well "? the reply is " Praise be to God "; and if two travellers meet and one asks the other "Where are you going?" he receives the reply "To the Gate of Bountiful God," after which the real errand may be discussed.

Just as " Inshaallah," literally meaning " If God wills," is really to be translated by a plain " Perhaps," so this habitual use of the phraseology and ordinances of religion, instead of indicating a living ever present influence, is here, as everywhere, the mark of easy formalism[1].

Only in the higher peoples, and quite recently in history, is moral perfection regarded as essential to religious pre-eminence, and so we find that, in general, a popular saint is venerated for his miracle working, and his moral worth, if any, is totally forgotten. But I wish to insist that this disregard of the holy man's morality is *not* a distinction of " savage " or " semi-heathen " men, but, shocking though it be, is common to all the lower moralities, of Europe or elsewhere, in the Middle Ages or the present time. I should explain also that

[1] I need not say that I refer to national habit. To say this of personal expression would be an obvious and gross libel.

until about seven years ago, when the first Arab shop-keeper settled in our village, the inhabitants did not know their prayers, the calls of the Muezzin or the performance of the worship known as "Mûled" described below. They called themselves Mohammedan, but knew nothing, and my friend the doctor says that the reply to his consolation to patients, "Well, you won't have this pain in Paradise," is often, "Who knows if there is a Paradise?"

On a sandy islet in the bay near my station, a spot of almost dreadful loneliness, is a shêkh's tomb of the simpler kind. The grave itself is surrounded by stones set on edge and the large white shells of *Tridacna,* and by a sort of hedge of sticks, the longer at the head, which the pious decorate with rags[1]. A second enclosure of stones includes this and the remains of other graves, and the whole area is kept perfectly clean and sprinkled with pure white sand from the beach. The short broken sticks and decayed rags are not thrown away, but carefully taken down and laid aside.

One is naturally interested to enquire who the Shêkh was in life, and what qualities are considered as meriting so much posthumous honour, and conferring the power of intercession with God. Strange to say, no one knows anything excepting that his name was Sad, the prevailing idea seeming to be that, since his usefulness and power began after his burial, there is no reason to be interested in who he was, and what he did, in life. Even after death but one miracle is vaguely recorded, viz. that a certain man attempted to steal some pearl shells which had been deposited at the grave, and so placed under the Shêkh's charge. The thief was punished by the loss of his hand, but whether by paralysis, or through the agency of a shark when he was diving, my informants neither knew nor cared. "It was something of that sort" was all they would say. And yet I believe that the dead

---

[1] It is curious how all races of mankind, from Ireland to India, Borneo, Japan and Zanzibar, should concur in decorating their holy places in this way. Probably practical convenience is a prosaic part of the explanation.

Plate XII

Fig. 22. Prayer at the grave of Holy Island

Fig. 23.   Note the shaven band over top of head distinctive of little boys ;
aristocrat on left wears a shirt and strings of amulets, the middle
one only a loin cloth and one lucky white stone

Shêkhs are more thought of as practical help in time of trouble than either God or the Prophet.

The once lonely tomb of Shêkh Barûd, whose name was in those days given to the harbour which is now Port Sudan, was mentioned in Chapter I. The name literally interpreted is "Old Man Flea," but it has no contemptuous significance to the pious. It was indeed a title of honour, for the old man so felt the sanctity of all life that he would not kill the most degraded of insects. His story is that of a poor pilgrim using all possible shifts to reach Mecca, and in the end succeeding. There are two accounts of his return. In the one he was compelled to trust himself to the sea journey of 180 miles alone in a tiny canoe. The sea spared him and he reached land where his tomb now stands, dying or dead of thirst. At any rate he was dead when found, and, being recognised as one who had perished on the pilgrimage, was buried as a shêkh. It is said that in memory of the manner of his death, sailors passing the spot pour a little fresh water into the sea. But, as a matter of fact, the custom is a general one, and all shêkhs' tombs are thus honoured. It is a fine example indeed of a persistent, widespread, and very ancient observance, probably less bound up with Moslem and old Christian theology than Omar Khayyam's well-known lines :

> "And not a drop that from our cups we throw
> For Earth to drink of but may steal below
> To quench the fire of anguish in some eye
> There hidden—far beneath and long ago."
> (See note by Aldis Wright in "Golden Treasury Edition.")

Personally I think my sailors are actuated by some quite vague sacrificial idea.

The second, and more correct, story places his death at Jedda, while on the pilgrimage. As those who die in the performance of this sacred duty earn very special merit, he was honoured by burial in a wooden coffin. During the ceremonies so violent a storm arose that the mourners left the coffin on the sea-shore. Next morning it was found that a sudden rise of the sea had borne away the saint, and later the coffin was found floated ashore at the entrance to a harbour on the other side of the sea[1]. When found it was recognised as the remains of a holy man, and buried in a stone tomb on high ground at the harbour entrance; which harbour was renamed after him, Mersa Shêkh Barûd. The harbour was then completely desert, and this tomb, the size of a very small room, was the only stone building, except two small police stations, between Suakin and Egypt! Once a conspicuous mark for sailors (the Government for this reason keeping it brightly whitewashed), it is now quite inconspicuous under the towering electric cranes and coal transporters of the modern seaport, of which it is the only object more than five years old.

The sites of the tombs of these Holy Men of a sailor people are always well and appropriately chosen, generally on high ground at a harbour entrance.   One I know, where the land is too low to give an impressive site, is built on the outermost point of the shore reef, hardly dry ground at lowest water level.   That of our Holy Island has been mentioned; that of Shêkh Dabadib is by a well, and is also a conspicuous mark on a coast otherwise featureless, even for the Red Sea.

Mohammedanism here meets Ancestor Worship and involves the sanctity of the head of a reigning house.   This tomb is none the less sacred for being new, antiquity and miraculous power are not always necessary to reverence. The Shêkh buried here is known to men still living, and his relatives are prominent people hereabouts.   The photograph shews the building, which contains the tomb, with a prayer-space

---

[1] In spite of its improbabilities the story illustrates well-known and interesting phenomena.   Such a sudden rise of the sea as is demanded is quite possible, and the shore level about Jedda, as elsewhere, is extremely low.   Though practically tideless the Red Sea is subject to variations of level which cannot be predicted, and which may be as much as three feet vertically.   Also objects from the Arabian shore are very commonly carried across the whole sea and stranded on the west side.   A year or two ago we learnt that abnormal floods had occurred in Arabia from the number of palm trunks found stranded, and another time, the whole coast, for 100 miles at least, was littered with the bases of palm leaves.   These had been left on the ground in some Arabian valley when the leaves were cut for use or sale, and carried into the sea by a flood.

Plate XIII

Fig. 24. A prophet that had honour in his own country

Fig. 25. A mediaeval tomb, now neglected

marked off outside, the Mecca-ward niche of which is decorated with flags. Here is also an almost perfectly spherical piece of granite, a natural boulder, black with libations of butter. One of my sailors is seen addressing this, hoping thereby to complete the prayers already made at the grave within.

The building of even so simple a tomb must have been a great expense so far from civilisation. Masons were brought from Suakin to trim the coral blocks, taken living from the sea, of which the walls are built.

The other photograph on this plate shews one of a series of little towers which are found here and there near the foot of the mountains, the finding of which, in the midst of a desert devoid of all buildings, is almost startlingly unexpected. They also are Moslem graves, but are not now regarded with reverence. Built long ago in the Middle Ages they are relics of the old trade route from the ancient kingdom of Axum, to the now vanished seaport of Aydeb which may some day be discovered in the ruins of "Old Suakin" or Berenice.

Another way of honouring the saints is by the killing of sheep at their graves, especially on feast days. The flesh is eaten of course—after being distributed to all who care to take it.

I suppose as a safeguard against idolatry the posture of prayer at a tomb is entirely different from those prescribed for prayer to God. There are no bowings, or kneelings with the forehead touching the ground. The petitioner stands throughout, holding the palms of his hands as though they were an open book from which he read, and at the end of his prayer passing them over his face. The idea symbolised is that during the prayer his heart is open to receive the blessing, and at the close his action sets forth his faith that a blessing has been received, and applied to his person.

Whenever in the desert men encamp for any length of time, a place is set apart for prayer, and marked off by stones set on edge. It is a semicircle or half oval, the apex of which is in the direction of Mecca, to which all the Moslems of the world turn to pray. The space within is kept clean as holy ground, and no one may step within the stones without first removing his sandals and washing, with water if by a well or the sea, otherwise with sand, as though entering a mosque.

The third type of religious exercise is the "zikr" or "remembrance," here called the "mûled[1]" or "Birthday," this name being given because the main part of the ceremonial is the reading of a long poem, composed by a shêkh of this country, describing the birth and life of Mohammed.

As in Egypt, religious recitation takes the place of a dinner party or evening entertainment. The material apparatus required are, first and foremost, lamps and candles, the more that can be borrowed the better; secondly, some carpets and sheets of matting to lay in a circle on the ground for the guests to sit upon. Minor matters are tea (coffee is more rarely used in our village) and incense.

Imagine the Eastern starlight relieving the soft purple darkness, a gentle moving air, cool after the heated storm winds of the day. The only light visible in the whole village is that placed before the reader, a brilliant little circle shewing up the principal guests in their white robes and turbans, the holy book and the smoking censer. One by one the guests appear out of the darkness, the droning chant of the reader taking no heed of their comings. Some, in new white robes and turbaned heads, or those to whom age gives dignity independently of wealth, seat themselves in the light near the reader; others, shaggy haired and wild faced herdsmen from the hills, in dust coloured calico, remain half seen on the farther side of the circle. No woman or girl is visible, but they may gather at a little distance and raise their curious whistling trill, their joy cry, at intervals. The little boys of the village, of the age at which church going and sitting still

---

[1] In Egypt Mûled or Mowled means a fair held on a saint's birthday. On the Red Sea coast a man "makes a mûled" to celebrate any private event, or simply by way of giving an entertainment.

generally were especially abhorrent to ourselves, are much in evidence, and certainly do not come for the tea, of which they may not be invited to partake.

The service contains real religious feeling, and besides the birth and life of Mohammed there is recited a long prayer, the droning of which is broken by the mournful chanting of responses, of which of course "La Allah ill' Allah" is one. Nothing could be more expressive of submission to the hardness of desert life, or so impress upon the listener remembrance of his exile from his fellows in the cheerful striving with life of the younger nations, than these people's singing, whether it be done for pleasure or as a religious service. The whole thing is full of Eastern poetic licence, e.g. blessings are called down upon each detail of the Prophet's body separately. At the point where his actual birth is announced all stand awhile. Only one sentence is really objectionable to a Christian, where all the older prophets extol Mohammed, Jesus is made to repeat the words of John, " I am not worthy to unloose his shoe latchet."

After about an hour's reading all rise and join hands in a circle, chanting "La Allah ill' Allah," "There is no god but God," emphasising the words with deep bowings, or by stamping the feet in unison ; after some repetitions the time quickens, and the sentence is shortened to "La Allah"; even these words are finally abbreviated to a grunt as the bowings and stampings degenerate into mere furious exertion. Another sentence repeated in the same way is "Hû hay kayâm," "He is the Life, the Almighty," with an emphasis on the pronoun, Hû, that excludes all sharers in His attributes. In the same way this sentence is shortened down to "Hu" alone, delivered with a deep gasp, so that at a little distance the sound of worship may be mistaken for the barking of dogs. At intervals one of the more excitable men enters and dances round inside the ring, urging the congregation to still greater rapidity and energy of sound and movement. When the men are tired they resume their seats, tea is handed round again, and more incense thrown on the charcoal, which is kept burning for the purpose. The reader resumes his recitation awhile until the spirit moves the congregation to rise, bow and repeat the formula " HE is the Life, the Almighty," as before.

The borderline between religion and superstition is of course very indefinite, and the belief in evil spirits and witch-craft is as strong as that in the intercession of dead saints. It is of no use to point out that such ideas are inconsistent with that of the Unity and Omnipotence of God, and only force can give weight to the consideration that loud drumming close to the head of a sick person, while certain to do harm, is unlikely to drive away the evil spirit which is the cause of the disease, or that a man suffering from heart disease is more likely to kill himself than drive out the evil spirit, by the violent exertions of a Mûled dance.

The wearing of amulets is, perhaps, the superstition most akin to religion, and one at least that has had its origin in intelligent respect for written wisdom. Every man wears them in numbers, and children have a few, mingled with other lucky objects, however insufficient their clothing. In the commonest form the paper is enclosed in a neat little leather case, a little over an inch square by half an inch deep, which may be slung round the neck with the prayer beads, by a string of twisted leather, or attached to a cord, of the same material, which passes round the arm just above the elbow. In some cases a man may wear up to twenty of these packets, partly as ornaments, partly as defence against each and all of the ills of life.

The contents are various, since, trusting to the ignorance of the purchaser, the charm-writer may put down the first thing that comes into his head, perhaps even lewd poetry, or the name of God written in various fantastic ways. Some charm-writers are quite illiterate, and their works are mere childish scribblings. A friend enquired of one of the better Shêkhs whether he had any faith himself in what he wrote, the reply being merely, " The Arabs like them so I write them." I suppose the corollary, "and I like the money they pay for them," may be taken for granted.

I was talking of amulets to one of my sailors. "The paper in this," he said, indicating a dingy silver case hung by a bit of string round his neck, "was worth four pounds." (This is two months' pay.) "When I was in Suakin I went to a shêkh there as I was ill. He was a great Fakir, a great Shêkh, and his tomb is now in the middle of the bazaar. He told me he had a very good paper by him, and if I wore it for twelve days, I should, if it pleased God, become well. The price of this paper was four pounds, but I said, ' I have only ten shillings.' ' Never mind,' said he, 'give me the rest if my words come true.' And after twelve days I got better. He was no liar." I was anxious to know whether the balance of the four pounds had been actually paid over or not, but my diplomatic questions were met by an impenetrable reserve, and the conversation was deflected into theology. "The Fakir does not say 'you must get better' after so many days, but only 'if it is God's will'."

The common way of dissolving the ink of the writing in water and drinking it as medicine, is practised here. Sometimes the fakir may instruct the patient to burn a piece of it each day on a censer, enclosing the smoke in his clothes and so fumigating himself with it. My clerk called on a sailor who was ill, or thought he was. The cause of illness was presumed to be the issue against him of a bad writing by some malicious person unknown, so the obvious cure was to get a counterblast written by someone friendly to the bewitched sufferer. Do not imagine the romance of oriental wizardry, or of mediaeval alchemists with patriarchal beards! Superstition is, in reality, most dingily matter-of-fact. The good fairy who wrote the counterblast is a fat, waddling, little man, with tiny screwed-up eyes in a face expressing only good-natured commonplaceness, as completely as his figure expresses laziness and love of food. He is in fact as much like a grocer as an eastern magician, but he is a good little man too, and has undertaken the work of village schoolmaster, and teaches the boys the correct bowings and postures of prayer, without any remuneration.

Customs, possibly peculiar to this people, and not held by the Arabs of the other side of the sea, for instance, are connected with milking. A woman may not milk a sheep or goat, only men may perform this duty. Further, a man having milked an animal may not drink until some other man, no matter whom, has first taken three sips. So strong is this idea that the phrase " He milks and drinks " is a term of abuse. One would think the origin of the custom to be the unwritten laws of hospitality, but if so, the present generation have no knowledge of any such derivation. " It is just the custom " is all they can say.

I remember meeting a little boy and his sister, who for this purpose had carried milk two miles or more, to the only house besides their father's then on the peninsula of Rawaya. What the thirsty father would have done if they had returned after finding no male at home I do not know. By chance one was ashore, the others having gone fishing.

Belief in the evil eye is universal here, as in the world at large, and the common sign which is supposed to afford protection against it, the figure of a hand with fingers outspread, is trusted in here also. This belief in the evil eye has prevented my obtaining more than one portrait of a woman, even the photograph of a woman's hand and rings, etc. (opp. page 24) being obtained with much difficulty. The lady stood within a little window, placed low down in the side of her house, so as to be quite satisfied that her head could not be " seen " by the camera's wicked glass eye. The reason *given* was that photography was an offence against their modesty, but I am sure the evil eye superstition had more to do with their reluctance.

The common idea that a pearl is due to the hardening of dew, to obtain which the oyster comes to the surface of the sea at night, was suggested to me by an Arab dealer, but a purely native idea is that abundance of rain in the winter will result in the appearance of many young oysters next summer. Because to themselves every drop of the scanty rainfall is precious beyond everything, they sympathetically imagine it must be of value to the oysters. However, this point, like the former on the formation of pearls, needs no great study of oyster habits to refute. As practically all oysters live under at least six feet of sea water, and are anchored firmly to the bottom, neither dew nor showers of rain can reach them, much less have any effect whatever upon them. Also the breeding season is summer, not winter.

The porpoise[1] is known as " Abu Salâma " or " Father of Safety," its useful habit, in days of long ago, being supposed to be the conveyance to shore of shipwrecked sailors. But one day, according to tradition, a porpoise rescued a negro, who, as soon as he reached shore, most ungratefully put a knife into poor Abu Salâma. Since that day shipwrecked mariners have had to shift for themselves. (Note how the blame is put on to the subject race. Prof. D'Arcy Thomson[2] gives a similar superstition regarding another kind of dolphin at Rio de Janeiro, where it is said to bring home the bodies of drowned sailors, and to defend swimmers against another genus which is dangerous to man.)

No one will destroy a cat or drown young kittens. This is not merely misplaced compassion or respect for life in general, as they bury[3] superfluous puppies without any qualm. Perhaps it is a relic of the ancient Egyptians' reverence for these animals. I tried to point out the inhumanity of allowing

---

[1] Really dolphin, but this name is also used for a certain fish. The true dolphins, like porpoises, are whales in miniature, air-breathing animals which have become disguised by a fish-like outer shape in accordance with their marine life. Internally every structure is like that of the land mammals from which they are descended, and totally different to that of fishes.

[2] *Science of the Sea*, issued by the Challenger Society, John Murray. Any reader interested in Part II of this volume should obtain this book as a guide to work in Marine Biology.

[3] One would not *drown* them simply because water costs money.

cats to multiply unchecked, and found that the avoidance of causing suffering to the cat had little, if anything, to do with the matter. "If they die of starvation it does not matter, but we must not kill them." The consequence is that every town and village swarms with miserable half-starved cats.

I was once staying in a house where the balcony, on which we dined, overhung the sea at a height of perhaps 30 feet. A miserable cat, which had adopted the house as her residence, came and made herself a nuisance by the usual feline methods. One of the guests rose, caught, and threw her over the balcony into the sea. It seemed rather callous, but obviously such an animal's destruction lessens the amount of misery in the world. I could hardly believe my eyes two days later, when that same cat walked on to the verandah. It appears that the process, which I had thought necessarily fatal, was repeated on this cat at recurring intervals, the dose being only sufficiently powerful to take effect for two or three days, after which she was as actively disagreeable as ever, and it had to be repeated.

Talking of cats there are not less than seven names for this one beast in Arabic! I wish I had taken down the complete list as my informant gave it, but one of the two I know is a good instance of onomatopœia, or instinctive naming from sounds associated with the object. The Arabic *gutt* is obviously the same as cat, and may be the same word by actual derivation, but the Red Sea word is " Biss," which, the Arab not being able to pronounce the letter P, is the same as " Puss." It is hard to believe that this should actually pass through Egypt to finally be used in England as a merely " pet" name. It must have arisen independently in the two countries.

Once travelling on the desert east coast of Zanzibar island and sleeping in the open, I awakened in the night to find an eclipse of the moon in progress (1901 was the year). I expected my boat boys to be alarmed at the phenomenon, especially as they were some of the original inhabitants of the island, not mingled with Arab blood. But they took it very calmly, saying something to the effect that "The English know all about that!" In my Red Sea village in 1909, it was quite different. On going out in the morning my clerk asked me whether I had been disturbed by the natives' efforts to save the moon's life, or, as he put it, Had I *heard* the eclipse? It appears that directly the shadow touched the moon everyone was aroused and a beating of tin cans commenced, with loud prayers that God would not allow the moon to be destroyed.

One of the origins of superstition is false reasoning from observed fact. When a native has a wound or open sore he is careful to keep his nose plugged with rag, or to sniff continually at aromatic substances, as he believes the smell of a wound will cause fever and mortification. The observation that if a wound smells, the patient is likely to be in a bad way, is sound enough, but the inference that the smell, or any smell, e.g. women's scents, causes the fever is superstition. I am informed that this idea is very widespread. I fear my applications of iodoform, than which nothing can have a more persistent smell, will convince the natives that we share their belief in the efficacy of "drowning," rather than preventing, the odour of decay.

Somewhat similar was the native treatment of a man who fell from the roof of a house we were building. He was lying senseless when I arrived, his nostrils carefully plugged with onion! Probably the smell of onion, like that of ammonia, may be useful in fainting, but far more important is free access of air, and *that* they treated as a matter of no account at all.

The great remedy for everything is the application of a red-hot nail. Hence many of the scars which otherwise might be taken for the results of fighting.

One of my men, being in great pain from stricture, I gave the maximum dose of opium for his relief. On returning to see the effect he answered, "Yes, I have had no pain since

they burned me." My little tabloids were despised as too
trifling a remedy for such serious ill; burning had been considered a more sensible treatment, and the relief afforded by
a full dose of opium attributed to it. " Perhaps it was the
English medicine that relieved your pain?" I suggested.
"The English medicine is good, but I have had no pain
since they burned me," he repeated. Great is Faith! How
many cures may have resulted from the faith excited by a
red-hot nail, without the aid of opium! At the same time
English medicines are highly valued, especially those which
have a prompt and visible effect, and there is no fear of their
being too nasty. I gave a baby girl, about a year old, a dose
of castor oil. She smiled and licked her lips; perhaps it was
no more unpleasant than native butter.

One of our camels fell lame. My clerk thought it had
stepped on a thorn, but the native opinion was that it had
smelled the dung of a hyaena.

A bundle of the knuckle bones of a sheep are hung up in
the tent with the object of assisting the healthy growth of the
baby, and dog's teeth are tied round its neck to insure the
regular succession of its own.

The cure for a headache is a string bound tightly round
the head, and amulets are generally included.

My junior clerk having been stung by a scorpion, was
induced by the severe pain, in the absence of other help, to
trust to native ministrations. His head (which has abundant
curly hair) they did with butter anoint, even with the mal-
odorous "samin," and gave him copiously of the same to
drink. The root of a certain tree was bound round his wrist
and an amulet round his elbow. I do not know which of
these four remedies effected the cure; a good drink of
"samin" would certainly have an effect in the right direction.

The Exhibit at Shepherd's Bush of "charms" and magical
objects, recently in use in England, indicates a mental level
no whit higher than that of my brown people. And yet with
what contempt would these English wearers of amulets and

dried mole's feet have regarded the "heathen niggers." And can we say much more for the large numbers of half-educated people who do not like to spill the salt, and generally bow to the new moon, because "there might be something in it," who refuse to believe what is strange to them, no matter what the evidence, though believing many things on no true evidence at all?

Religion and superstition having occupied so much of our attention, I seem to lack a sense of proportion in devoting but a short space to the more real matter of morality. Brevity is, however, excused by the fact that all description of men's ways of life is necessarily an exposition of their moral state.

These northern tribes, isolated in the deserts, possess the primitive, yet most advanced, virtue of strict honesty. During the winter, when rain has fallen upon certain favoured spots and most of the population has migrated to them, one frequently comes across small trees bearing bundles of matting, boards, and sticks, the materials of a tent-house. The owner has left the country for the time the grazing will last, and, not wishing to take all his house with him, merely puts the materials out of the reach of the goats, secure in finding them untouched, not even borrowed, on his return two or three months later; this too in a country where even a bit of old sacking is a thing of value.

CHAPTER IV

THE DAILY LIFE OF THE PEOPLE

At first sight, the country seems to be one from which no human being could extract the barest subsistence. The usual explanation, that the natives live by stealing, did not help me to an understanding, as that is no more an economic possibility than the story of the two old women who lived by taking in each other's washing. The fact is, the Sudan sheep, goats and camels, have a marvellous tenacity of life, and on their sufferings the native exists. I once had acquaintance with a British donkey to whom corn was given on a piece of stiff brown paper, to prevent waste. When the corn was done, the donkey proceeded to eat the brown paper before going to his desert of thistles. What luxury a diet of brown paper and thistles would be to a Sudan goat! After nibbling dry sticks all day in the desert, they come and eat resinous shavings from my workshops, or pick up single grains of corn from the sand where our camels have been fed, shewing that a day's feeding leaves them ravenous beyond all the British donkey's idea of hunger.

My particular village is richer than most places on the coast in possessing a few square miles of scattered acacias which bear a few little leaves when all else fails. There are some salt woody plants too (Arabic, *hamid* = sour) and some low trees ("Asal" or "adlib") which are a vivid green all the year round, the latter of which, however, all animals, except camels, refuse.

The goats spend much of their day on their hind-legs, supporting themselves with their fore-legs on the lower

Plate XIV

Figs. 26 and 27.   Water carriers.   Three to five full skins are slung
over a wooden saddle, the odd one balanced on the top

branches of the acacias while reaching as high as their necks will stretch to nibble the little leaves from among the inch-long and needle-sharp thorns. I have even seen goats standing with all four feet on boughs several feet above the ground. This is a fairly uncomfortable way of living, indeed I should think the most diligent browsing, and the most callous disregard of the contact of lips and tongue with thorns, would scarcely keep a healthy goat's stomach full. But it is better than the alternative, the hurried pacing with short stops just long enough to eat the single blades of dry grass, which is the only food should the locusts come down and clear every leaf off the acacias. I speak glibly of single blades of dry grass, but I am far too optimistic in my terms. A scrap of woody salt herb, or a bit of grass-stick, something like slender bamboo, is all that is visible to the human eye. For some months they graze on hope, air and dust, and are given a very minute ration of "dûra" corn on their return home in the afternoon. (This dûra, *Sorghum vulgare*, is called darri seed at home, and is used only for fowls I believe.) Why is the camel the only type of endurance? Surely the goat is his equal? As for drinking, goats are not watered oftener than camels, and in both cases water too salt and filthy for human beings is good enough for them.

In the winter and spring, *if* it rain, things are better; a little thin grass appears, single blades which last only a week or two, and the grey-brown tufts of sticks, which are the remains of last year's grass hummocks, put forth scanty leaves and long wiry stems, a little less dry than those they spring from. The sour "hamid" becomes brilliant and luxuriant, and the acacias more leafy than usual. The beds of the torrents, which contain water only for a short time immediately after rain, become in some places almost full of grass, though at the best there is always much more sand and gravel than vegetation to be seen, except in the most favoured spots.

A large number of annuals of the clover tribe appear in some places, for instance in the valleys of the raised coral ground of Rawaya peninsula; in consequence, after it has rained, there is a small exodus from our village, and boats are employed to convey families, tents and animals across the bay, to stay there so long as the water supply will last.

It is astonishing that the acacias and "hamid" can struggle through the climatic conditions and the incessant persecution of the animals. Think of their young trees wholly at the mercy of the famishing goats, who every year eat even the hamid nearly to bare sticks. The women again beat the trees to obtain the leaves which are out of reach of the animals, and collect particularly the flowers and green seed pods in this way. Somehow the acacia still struggles on, producing leaves and flowers even after a rainless winter. The hamid seems to be able to live on dew, for it puts forth new shoots and becomes green in the spring independently of rain.

Very few natives are so tied down to any village as to be dependent on a local rainfall. If rain is seen to fall for an hour or so in any direction for several days in succession, they have only to make a bundle of their tent and cooking-pot and be off to the favoured spot. Even beyond the limits of their tribal districts the whole desert is home; there are no fixtures in it other than the wells. Inland there are no permanent villages; indeed, in the north country, it is rare to see more than two or three tents together. Even in the fixed villages of the coast and the considerable suburbs of Suakin about Shâta, the majority of the habitations are tents, and most of their owners are there only for part of the year to buy corn until the rain comes again[1].

Every year my men have leave to go, one or two at a time, to visit their relatives. A hundred miles' journey to search for persons whose whereabouts he knows extremely

[1] Suakin is populous in winter, the inhabitants going into the hills to escape the summer heat. At my village the reverse is the case.

vaguely, and who are continually moving, is nothing to the native, even though he may do all, or nearly all, afoot. Only once has a man come back to report that he had tramped all his three weeks' leave away without coming across those he sought. Not family affection only prompts these visits, though I believe that feeling is strong in most cases. They desire to drink milk, as they put it, rightly believing that a diet of rice and dûra needs the addition of milk for a month or two in the year if health is to be preserved. This is especially the case with the men in my employ who are often either those who possess few animals or who have made over their flocks to relatives.

This desert is a great camel-breeding area. For travel or military purposes the camel bred in Egypt and fed on juicy clover is obviously useless, so, every spring, representatives of the Coast Guards and Slavery Repression Department come down from Egypt to buy. As a good camel is worth £12 to £18 the man who has a couple to sell is sure of enough money for himself and his family to live on for a year. The milk of the females is a source of food.

An article made in considerable quantities in the country is butter, so called, or samin to give it its native name. It is a whitish liquid with a powerful cheesy smell, repulsive to the European. The native regards it as one of the necessities of life; I have known sailors leaving for a week's voyage to turn up next day with "we forgot our samin" as their excuse for returning. This is, to their minds, as good a reason as if they had forgotten the rice, the water, and the matches as well [1].

The nomads' tents are illustrated opposite the next page. Externally they are made of palm-leaf matting [2], in colour as well as in shape suggesting haycocks. The sheets of this

---

[1] Flint and steel are sometimes used, but nowadays matches are extremely cheap in all corners of the world.

[2] The leaves and midribs of the date palm are essentials to the people of the desert, nowadays at least, as they use them for all sorts of handicrafts. There are some date palms near Suakin, but their matting is imported.

material are stretched over long, bent sticks and fastened together with wooden skewers. The doorway of the tent is on the less steeply-sloping side and though only two or three feet high is partly curtained with a piece of sacking or other cloth. They are invariably built with their backs to the north, that is, against the prevailing wind. This is the case even in the summer, when to be out of the wind is torture to the European. If the wind changes to the south, the door is closed up and the wall propped up a little on the north side. In all, except the poorest, the house is divided into two parts, even though the whole space is generally only about 10 feet square. The larger division is formed by the erection of a kind of second tent of goat's hair cloth within that of matting. This is entirely closed in by a curtain from the low space by the doorway where the cooking is done, and where visitors sit on their heels.

The inner compartment is really a sort of four-poster family bed, the bed and bedding consisting of some boards arranged as a flooring a few inches above the ground, on which is spread a mat made of the split midribs of palm-leaves placed parallel to each other and tied together with thin strips of leather. This is known as the "serîr," a word which in Egypt denotes a bedstead. For bedding there is perhaps a hard leather pillow, or a piece of rough log will serve this purpose. I have seen odd ends of squared poles thrown away from some carpenter's shop used thus, for sharp angles in the pillow are not regarded by men whose idea of comfort is a plank bed minus blankets.

If a regular bedstead be part of the furniture of a town house, it is an "angarîb" made of cords stretched over a frame. This, if large and well made, is very comfortable, judged even by European standards.

Of the other objects to be seen in the house the most conspicuous is the master's shield, with dagger belt and sword, and the most essential is a large water jar. To one of the upright sticks supporting the tent are hung various

Plate XV

Fig. 28. Tents on the edge of Yemêna Oasis

utensils containing the family larder, e.g., the bowls and skins of milk (which is generally sour and evil smelling). The milk bowls are curious, being either closely woven, water-tight baskets of palm-leaf, gourds[1], or bottles hollowed out of solid blocks of hard wood. Some of these latter are great works of art, being perfectly round and nearly as thin as porcelain vessels, though cut out of a dark red wood entirely by the unaided hand. The practical advantages of enamelled iron ware appeal to the natives ; the brass cooking pots of antique design, such as shewn in Fig. 50 on Plate XXIII, and the fellows of which may be seen at Pompeii, are being replaced by this prosaic material. For cups, empty meat tins, cleaned and the edges straightened, are most commonly used if an European lives near. A stock of samin butter may be kept in a four-gallon paraffin tin.

Of all the kindly fruits of the earth the onion is the greatest boon to us desert dwellers. Its portability and keeping qualities enable it to arrive fresh and wholesome even at this end-of-the-world village, and after weeks of rice and dûra diet the value of a dish flavoured with onions is immense. It is the only vegetable ever used, water-melons being the only fruit, and those but rarely seen even in the winter.

Smoking is rather rare, chewing universal. Pipes or "hubble-bubbles" I have not seen except in the hands of Egyptians or Arabians, the tobacco being burnt by natives in the end of a piece of sheep's marrow-bone, or as cigarettes. All love to chew a kind of brown snuff which seems to be a great solace during work and in the intervals of pearl diving.

Tea is taken after every meal and oftener. A half-pint teapot suffices for half a dozen men as it is sipped, saturated

---

[1] Gourds are continually mentioned in books of travel, and as the word remained mysterious to me from my eighth to my twentieth year I explain in detail. Certain species of melon-like plants produce a hard-skinned fruit, the bitter pulp of which dries up to a powder, leaving the skins hollow. Cut a hole in this, clear out the seeds and fibre, and you have a basin or a bottle according to the shape of the fruit. Only the former shape is seen on the Red Sea coast.

with sugar, from tiny glass tumblers.   Its flavour, poor to begin with, is utterly spoiled by the brackish water and of course by the excess of sugar.

Coffee is not so much used in our village, though in the South I was told by a resident Egyptian official, "These people do not complain if they have no food.   They are used to that, but if they have no coffee they become as though mad." Coffee is made in the following manner :—Glowing charcoal is placed in a thick wooden bowl (*a*) of Fig. 31, the "beans[1]" laid upon it, and the whole shaken occasionally to keep the charcoal alight and yet prevent burning.   When roasted, the berries are pounded in a wooden mortar (*b*) with a stone pestle (*c*).   The wooden case and its cover (*d*), like the rest, is cut out of solid wood and contains the fragile earthenware coffee pot.   The coffee is boiled in this until it froths up, when the pot is removed until it subsides, when it is replaced on the fire and removed until it has frothed up three times. After it has been allowed to settle for a minute or two it is ready to sip[2].

Incense is used, not only during religious performances, but also for scenting the clothes and body.   The man or woman desiring this luxury squats over a smouldering censer, which he covers with the clothes he is wearing, so that all the smoke is collected within them.

Some form of citron oil is used very extensively as a scent, indeed so much so that the odour of it seems characteristic of natives.   Possibly some of its favour is due to its usefulness in keeping off mosquitoes.

Except for the liberal anointing of the hair with mutton fat, the natives are very cleanly in their persons, and quite free from vermin.   The sailor population is so much in the sea as well as on it that they could hardly be dirty; but I

---

[1] Is "coffee bean" a corruption of the Arabic *bûn*?

[2] This is of course the regular way of making Turkish coffee and can be imitated at home by anyone.   The coffee should be finely ground or crushed like cocoa.

Plate XVI

Fig. 29. Goats feeding on thorn bushes

Fig. 30. Milk bowls, plaited and wooden, gourd and baskets

      d   *b*   *a*

                c

Fig. 31. A coffee set, and some women's rings

Plate XVII

Fig. 32. Arabian sword dance

Fig. 33. Arabian sword dance

Fig. 34. Hamitic wedding dance

believe all natives will wash when they can.   Inland, I am informed, things are very different, but there the preciousness of water is an all sufficient excuse.   It is one recognised by their religion, which permits dry sand to be used for water in the ablutions necessary before prayer in the desert.

Set forms of amusement seem to be few.   As already mentioned, the performance of the Mûled is both a religious exercise and an entertainment, and a peculiar " dance " is indulged in with much relish on all occasions, though the performance seems pointless and monotonous in the extreme. The photograph was taken at a wedding, the bundle of dried palm leaves on the extreme left set up on the ridge pole of the tent being here, where no palm trees grow, the symbol of wedded prosperity.   The women guests form a rough semicircle and provide music by chanting and clapping the hands together.   The men stand in a group opposite at a little distance, and at intervals one or two of them run forward towards the women, jump into the air as high and as often as they can, and then return to their fellows.   The photograph shews two men at the top of their jump together.

The sword dance illustrated was a really fine display, made by the captain and crew of a merchant *sambûk* which was in harbour.   Hearing a considerable noise in the village one night, I strolled out to see what it might be, and found complete silence and darkness !   Enquiring at the house of one of my sailors, I found the whole party in his tiny hut ; I told them there was not the least objection to their dance provided it went on no longer than midnight, and that I should much enjoy seeing it.   I was rewarded by a really interesting display, instead of the tame performance I expected ; sticks being used in place of swords.   So I arranged for another performance, which is depicted on Plate XVII, by daylight, and gave leave for real swords to be brought from the *sambûk*.   The principal dancers each had a sword and its scabbard in their hands, the crew, negro and Arab, forming the lines between which the dancers marched, turned and whirled to the sound of song, clapping and drum. It was desperately hot work by daylight, but the enjoyment of all is visible even in the photograph.

Sham fights are sometimes performed, with apparent fury, by natives armed with sword and shield; but this is a much lower thing than the symbolic expression of emotion given by the Arabians' dance. The ordinary negro dancing is absolutely stupid in appearance, and I could not find that the performers attached any meaning to it. Two of these men, however, can give a good sham fight with sticks, but it is that and nothing more, the emotions dramatised being of the crudest. Throwing their heavy curved walking sticks at another which is stuck vertically into the sand, is one of the minor amusements for boys and men. Sides are chosen, the losers' penalty is to carry the winners on their backs over the range, or this may be compounded for by the losers standing cups of tea. This is really practising a useful art, as hares &c. are killed in this way. There is also a game in which two men move white and black pebbles over a draughtboard in which holes are cut to contain the pebbles, or the board may be merely a series of little holes in the sand. There is a good deal of gambling over cards, the ordinary European cards, and those of good quality too, being very cheap. I was at pains to discover the game, but found it so elementary and uninteresting that I straightway forgot it again. Perhaps this is why it is played for money; without serious gambling interest the game would not be worth playing, even to a native.

CHAPTER V

SAILORS OF THE RED SEA

THE sailors of the Red Sea are practically all Arabians and their negro slaves. They generally give Jedda or a neighbouring port as their headquarters, though some are from Sinai in the north to Hodêda in the south. The Sudan coast is merely a portion of their beat, few vessels really belong to the country. The pearlers, too, come and go as they visit the reefs of the whole sea in turn.

The maritime Hamites are so very few and so rarely depend entirely on the sea for a living, but upon their animals also, that it is surprising to find that they are distinguished in any way from the country population. The difference may be expressed in the actual words of one of them. " You see that man riding a camel? He would think me a fool because I know little about camels, while I think him a fool because he might die of hunger by the sea-side, not knowing how to get even clams (*Tridacna*) to eat."

" When these people from the hills come down here and we offer them rice they look at it and say 'That is worms (? maggots), we don't eat worms.' "

They are skilful sailors of their little dug-outs and readily learn the management of larger vessels, but very rarely go with the Arabians away from their own coast. No boat building is done even in Suakin, the country being devoid of timber, though repairs can be effected there.

The coasting vessels of the Red Sea are "dhows" or as here named "sambûks" (see Figure on pages 60 and 62, and Fig. 36, Plate XVIII). Several kinds are distinguished by separate names, e.g. a rather small type is known as a "gatîra," but all are essentially the same. They are both beamy and deep, with long overhanging bow and a square stern. There is little keel apart from the depth of the boat itself and they are not good at beating to windward. They are quite open, such decking as there is at bow and stern being merely for convenience in managing sail and rudder, not built with the idea of protection from a sea breaking aboard.

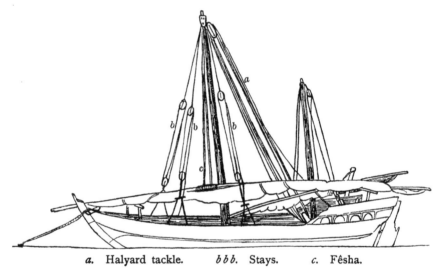

a. Halyard tackle.　　*b b b.* Stays.　　*c.* Fêsha.

Fig. 37. Rigging of a *sambûk*

The rig is a single lateen sail of cotton canvas, which in a boat over 50 feet long is of great size. A mizzen mast is stepped, but the mizzen sail is only used under the very best of conditions. I have often asked the headman of one of these boats why, on starting out with a light breeze at 6 o'clock in the morning he did not set his mizzen, and have been told that, as he knew the breeze would freshen about 10 a.m., it was not worth while. They are excellent sea boats and will stand a great deal of bad weather. Despite the extreme clumsiness of the rig and the apparently haphazard way the

Plate XVIII

Fig. 35. Pearling canoes coming in from diving

Fig. 36. A pilgrim *sambûk*

numerous half-naked sailors tumble over one another and yell like Babel when anything has to be done, they are cleverly handled. When travelling in them I have sometimes seen situations calling for an extreme nicety of manipulation to avoid an accident, manœuvres which were carried through with skill and coolness by men who, placed in an English boat, would seem both clumsy and mentally unbalanced.

Besides the clumsiness of the lateen rig with its huge single yard, the primitive blocks and tackle used necessitate a large crew. One of my boats, 50 feet long by 10 feet beam, requires a crew of nine, and the headman considers this too few. Generally all passengers join heartily in the hauling

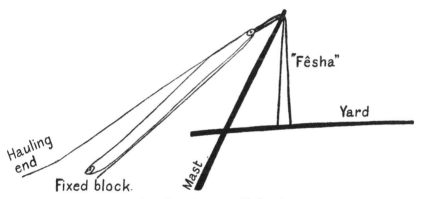

Fig. 38. Diagram of halyard

and yelling, which (especially the latter) is necessary to raise the great yard. Two thick ropes, named the Fêsha, attached to the yard pass through rough sheaves at the mast head, the other ends being both attached to a hanging pulley block of four sheaves or more. Through the sheaves of this hanging block pass the halyards, which, running through a block at deck level form a tackle by which the hanging block and the "fêsha" ropes are hauled down and the yard of course rises. In practice there are two halyards, both passing through the same hanging block, as there is not room for the whole crew to haul at a single rope. The cordage is all made of coconut fibre and there is no standing rigging, all stays and the "vang," or stay to the yard, being moveable and set up with simple tackles. They may be made very useful in hauling heavy goods aboard when loading.

There are two principal disadvantages of this lateen rig which call for special skill. The first is that at the end of each tack in a head wind you cannot "go about" in the ordinary way but must *fall away* from the wind and wear round. In an ordinary fore and aft rigged vessel this operation would involve gibing, the sail going over with a violent bang which would be extremely dangerous in a high wind, especially where the tack of the sail is fixed down forward of

Fig. 39. Laden *sambûk* under sail
(*From a photograph*)

the mast. As this sail has no boom gibing is avoided by letting go the sheet and carrying it and the sail forward while the tack is unfastened and brought aft, both meeting at the mast, so that the sail is practically furled. The long yard, being balanced by its suspension at the mast head, is brought to a vertical position, the sheet carried forward of both it and the mast and so round to its new position on the other side and carried aft. As there is no tackle[1] on either sheet or tack the boat is so steered as to help these movements and

[1] The sheet is passed round a smooth thick thwart and one or two of the crew take up the slack as the rest haul in. This *to some extent* takes the place of tackle.

the sail does not draw until the sheet is made fast. It is to facilitate the movement of the heavy yard from one side of the mast head to the other that the mast slopes forward so markedly. The operation is ingenious and calls for good seamanship, especially in a strong wind and heavy sea, when any fault might result in great force being unexpectedly applied to the rigging with awkward results. Just as this is the reverse to our gibing so, instead of carrying weather helm, the vessel falls off from the wind instead of luffing if left to herself, and where the steersman of a fore and aft rigged vessel would luff to a big wave or strong squall the Arabian falls away. As there is but one sail, a large part of which is forward of the mast while the deepest part of the keel is aft, it is impossible to have any of the sail set when at anchor, and so the anchor must be raised, sail set and way got on the vessel almost simultaneously, indeed the sail must draw as soon as it begins to rise and the yard is not at the mast head till some distance has been travelled. Similarly on coming into harbour the sail is lowered completely, long before the anchorage is reached.

Like most sailors of the warmer seas the Arabs are amphibious. For instance, the order is given to carry out an anchor away from the vessel, which is to be moved by hauling on the anchor rope. If the distance is not great and the depth inconsiderable the sailors will consider it less trouble, instead of lowering a canoe in which to carry out the anchor and rope, to throw them overboard and then go after them with a run, a yell and splash, to the sea bottom, where two or three men seize and run with the anchor a few yards under the water, come up for a breath of air while others go down, descend again and carry the anchor another stage, until the anchor rope is fully extended. Generally when the anchor goes overboard at the end of the day's journey one or two of the crew go down after it and work it nicely into the mud. Similarly in getting an anchor up if it is caught in the coral, instead of manœuvring the boat to loosen it in the

usual way a man goes down to see what is the matter, and
either loosens it or directs the operations of those in the boat.
How would an English yachtsman regard diving after his
anchor ? Not as an everyday occurrence, but as an adventure
of a lifetime.

To the Arab sailors such a voyage as from Bombay to
Aden, and on through the whole length of the Red Sea, must
be an adventure like that of a voyage of Ulysses. As to the
old Hero so to them all accidents are due to the personal
intervention of God, or of good and evil spirits, and there is
no dividing line between fact and legend. Distances, which
for us have so dwindled, remain for them enormous. I have
myself spent as long over a voyage of a hundred miles,
anchoring each night in yet another desolate creek or "khor,"
as over the whole voyage by steamship from Marseilles to
Port Sudan. At that rate 1000 miles in a *sambûk* would be
almost equivalent to a circumnavigation of the globe in a
modern vessel. But what a difference ! In the latter case,
to the passenger deck chairs and novels, to the officers
methodical routine and the keeping the running correct as
per time-table, in the former ceaseless personal effort, at
frequent intervals the direct pitting of oneself against the
chances of the sea, the winds and waves, reefs and hidden
coral pinnacles, the everyday hardship often aggravated by
the rarity of the points at which water and food may be
procured. Rarely are two days alike, and the date of the
voyage's close is, as they would express it, known to God.
And adventures everywhere, the calling at strange little
desert towns, the outer fringe of even Arabian and Turkish
civilisations, islands and harbours unknown to the outer world,
wild peoples, communities living apart, connected with the
world only by some rudiments of their common faith, savages
even to the Arab sailors. There is too, even yet, the chance
of meeting pirates, or of a windfall or ruin resulting from
some smuggling adventure. I would that they could be
conscious of the poetry of it all. To them the glory of the

Plate XIX

Fig. 40. Hamitic fisherman

Fig. 41. A small pearling *gatîra*

Fig. 42. A large pearling *sambûk* with ten canoes

battle is but the hardship of everyday life, strange scenes and places only the possible failure to procure provisions or the chances of being robbed by petty tyrants. At least it is a life that makes real men, men who must have learned some communion with the God of Nature and the Sea.

The Hamites are skilful sailors of their small boats and of the little dug-out canoes in which pearl fishing is done. These measure about 16 ft. in length with a beam of 18 in. to 2 ft. For a short distance weather seems to be of no consideration to them; one sees canoes tearing along under full sail, the steersman busy throwing out[1] the water with his spare hand, while the other occupant hangs to the mast which threatens to be carried away by the wind at every moment, and leans as far over the side as he can to prevent her capsizing. I know several cases of men travelling eighty to a hundred miles along the coast in such canoes, partly on the open sea and partly on the shallow water over the reefs. One instance is particularly remarkable, a bent old man, practically blind with age, appeared, having travelled from the next village to the north, eighty miles away. His only companions were two particularly irresponsible-looking little boys, whose ages I should estimate at 8 and 10. I enquired how he managed the boat seeing he was blind. "The boys tell me to luff or bear away and I do as they say" he replied, as if that were quite a simple, safe, and easy method of travel.

Pearl fishing is carried on by the Arabs all over the Red Sea by means of vessels of every size from the smallest, carrying four men and a boy, to the largest with a crew of twenty or more. Frequently the captain is a patriarch, the crew being largely his family and connections, with a few negro slaves or ex-slaves.

The *sambûk* carries as many canoes, dug out of solid tree trunks, as it can, up to half the number of the crew, and the

---

[1] They do not *bale* water out of a canoe, but *throw* it with a paddle, shell or broken wooden bowl! The method is very effective.

actual fishing is done from these canoes, the large vessels being merely means of transport and eating and sleeping places.

On reaching the fishing-ground the *sambûk* anchors, under the shelter of a reef, perhaps miles out to sea, or perhaps near some islet or sandbank. The canoes with which it is loaded are launched and two men paddle away in each. Though both can dive they go in pairs distinguished as "captain" and "paddler," the former being chosen for good eyesight and skill in distinguishing the pearl shells from the weeds, sponge, and stones among which they grow. A bad captain "sees every stone as a shell" which results in waste of energy in useless diving. He examines the sea-bottom by means of a "water telescope" (Arabic "Maraya," a word also applied to mirrors, among other things), a paraffin tin with a glass bottom. The glass is pressed on the surface of the sea, thus flattening out ripples and giving a smooth surface through which, in this transparent sea, objects can be clearly seen at a depth of from twenty, thirty, and sometimes even sixty feet[1]. So the canoe is slowly paddled over the sea until a shell is sighted, when the canoe is manœuvred into the proper position, and the diver descends and secures it. The business is not generally a simple dive and return, though that is a clever enough thing to do without upsetting the canoe. In the case of not quite fully-grown oysters the creature is attached to the bottom by a very strong silky green cable, and I have watched the diver plant both feet firmly on the bottom, and wrench and twist at the sharp-edged shell with both hands for some time before it would come away.

The average duration of a long dive is 90 seconds, two minutes being the longest I have seen. To one in the boat counting the seconds waiting for the reappearance of the diver this seems a long time, and doubtless the exaggerated reports of divers staying under water for five minutes have

---

[1] Merely to see the bottom, without distinguishing small objects, is often possible at greater depths still.

Plate XX

Fig. 43. A pearl oyster seen ; manœuvring the canoe

Fig. 44. The dive

Fig. 45. The "oyster" secured

Fig. 46. Landing on Dongonab beach

thus arisen. Two minutes of considerable exertion under the pressure of 30 ft. of water is surely a sufficiently remarkable feat. The greatest depth to which a naked diver descends is thirteen fathoms, equal to seventy-eight feet.

The captain only dives for an hour or two in the morning, after which he saves his eyes for finding the shells which his paddler secures. These men, whether Arabs of the *sambûks* or Hamites who go out from their villages in canoes, dive without any apparatus at all. A few negroes descend by a weight and cord in likely places where the water is too deep to see the bottom, on the chance of coming across shells. The Hamites ridicule them for using this method, but so far as I can see their results are just as profitable. Two or three large shells seem to be considered an adequate reward for a day's great labour.

The provisions for a *sambûk's* cruise of six months are of the simplest, sacks of dûra corn and a barrel or two of the brackish warm water of the desert wells. Stones for grinding the corn, a big cooking-pot and a basin or two are the whole equipment. The fire is kindled on a box of sand. A sheep kept alive until a feast day, is sometimes seen on board, but coffee is the one luxury. It is a terribly hard life. Think of coming in from a day's work of diving and paddling a canoe under that blazing sun to a meal of tasteless dûra porridge, sometimes a little fish, burnt rather than cooked[1], and warm brackish and dirty water, eaten probably without shelter from the sun, or at best under a scrap of flimsy cotton, here set against a sun which blazes and scorches rather than shines. Well have they earned their night's rest, yet what a bed is theirs, a surface of hard wood without even the flatness and smoothness of the plank bed of a prison cell.

Though sharks occur and are sometimes common in the Red Sea, a native does not look round for them before going

---

[1] The flesh of the pearl oysters and clams are only eaten when all else fails and as fish is obtainable in times of scarcity it is not much appreciated when anything else is to be had.

overboard, though if one should be seen, diving is over for the day. To one locality, named Shark Island, divers will not go for fear of these beasts, but diving is continually going on in a bay where several sharks are captured each year. I have only heard of one fatality, in which case a man's feet were taken off and he bled to death after regaining his canoe.

Fishing is done by running a net round a shoal of fish, by throwing-net, hook and line, trolling with a scrap of white rag or sheepskin with white wool left on, and by spearing. The latter method alone is peculiar to this coast so far as I know, so the former need but scant mention. The throwing-net is circular, about twelve feet in diameter, made of fine string with small mesh. The circumference is weighted with small pieces of lead. In use the fisherman grasps the centre of the net and folds the rest over his arm carefully, after wringing out excess of water. He then walks cautiously along by sandy shallows, looking for the ripplings, invisible to foreign eyes, which indicate the movements of fish. On seeing these, bending double, he creeps up as cautiously as possible until near enough to throw. This is done very suddenly and with a circular motion, so that the net spreads out parachute fashion in the air and descends vertically upon the fleeing fish. The fisherman kills any that are enclosed by biting their heads through the meshes of the net before removal. The fish thus captured is generally a species of mullet about the size of a herring, and excellent on the table. Its native name is El Arabi, i.e. the Arab. The method is of course only possible in shallow water with a sandy bottom, but such ground occurs at the head of all the harbours, so the throwing-net is much used. I have seen two men returning from fishing with festoons of "Arabs" covering their whole bodies, but such good luck as this is not common.

Hook and line fishing is the same here as anywhere else. The favourite baits are "sardines" and pieces of the flesh of the giant clam (*Tridacna*) or of the big whelks (*Fusus*, *Murex*, and *Strombus*), all of which are as easily obtained as lug-worms or mussels at home. Clams' flesh is the commonest, and anyone interested in curio-collecting should ask a fisherman to keep for him the pearls found in them. As the clam shell is an opaque white, so are the pearls, which, though consequently valueless, are as much true pearls as those formed by the lustrous pearl oyster.

"Sardines" are known even to the natives by this name, but are a small species of anchovy of the sardine size. At certain times they collect, presumably for breeding purposes, into shoals in the shallow water so dense as to form black patches 10 or 20 yards across, from which it is easy to collect a bucket-full in a few minutes by means of a sheet. They are kept alive by the fisherman allowing his canoe to be a third full of water in which they swim until thrown overboard to attract fish, or impaled on the hook as bait.

The number of species of fish thus caught is large and the greater number are very good. The best are several species of *Caranx* known as "bayâda," some of which attain to a great size, sometimes four or five feet long, but the smaller are better for eating. The most peculiar is perhaps the "abu sêf" or "father of a sword," a most appropriate name. It is ribbon-shaped, three feet long or so, back and belly quite straight and flattened from side to side, in fact just the shape of a sword blade. Further, its sides are of the most dazzling whiteness, brighter than any silver, and its ferocious teeth and vigorous movements bring the terror of a sword to all the smaller fish.

The nets and spears bring in the greatest variety of all, the brilliant blue, pink, and green species of the parrot-beaked *Pseudoscarus*, which actually eat coral; the queer bladder-fish, in which also the teeth are fused up like beaks, which can blow themselves up like footballs, in one species (*Tetraodon hystrix*) thus erecting the hundreds of fearful spines into which its scales are modified; the box or coffer fish, the skins of which are quite stiff and bony and cover square bodies, which in some species have horn-like spikes pointing forward over the eyes; file fish (*Ballistes*) which feed by crunching up shellfish (including pearl oysters) with their powerful jaws; in fact enough variety of strange habits and shapes and colours, striking by their brilliance or interesting by their resemblances to the inanimate environment of their possessors, to fill another book (were half known) or stock a museum.

Besides fish of ordinary size the larger species, such as rays and sharks, are generally captured by spearing. Nowadays the spear is a piece of round bar iron, half an inch in diameter, a rough unbarbed point at one end and with an eyehole, to which a line is attached, at the other. It is twelve feet long, and quite small fish may be impaled upon it in twenty-four feet of water. Its use is often combined with pearl fishing. Should the captain see a fish the spear is handed to him as he leans over the side of the canoe, and he watches the fish through the water glass in one hand, the spear being held in the other, with perhaps half its length in the water, more or less according to the depth. The canoe being rightly placed, a sudden jerk sends the spear shooting downwards, and more often than not the fish is impaled at the first attempt; so little splash is there, that it is often possible to throw it several times without driving the fish away altogether.

There are in most tropic seas certain gigantic rays or skates, whose horizontally flattened bodies are like a huge square, ten to twenty feet across. One corner is the head, eyes above, mouth underneath, the two side corners are fins, while to the fourth is attached the tail. This is a strange thing for a fish, being like a whip-lash, say 6 feet long, provided at its base with one or more erectile spikes four to six inches long, sharp and barbed all along each edge, and further very poisonous. The natives of both Zanzibar and the Red Sea assure me that even in the case of the smaller species, to tread on these spikes is death. Hence the common name of the family, Sting Rays. It is interesting to note that these dangerous implements are used purely in self-defence. All species are conspicuously coloured, one being yellow brown

Plate XXI

Fig. 47.   Pearl-divers

with large bright blue spots, another black with round white spots. The largest are black, and so conspicuous on the sandy bottoms they frequent that none but the most unteachable animal, human or otherwise, can incur the dreadful penalty of careless interference with them. Otherwise the animals are perfectly harmless, living on shellfish which their small but powerful jaws can crush up[1]. Yet so impressive is the size of some species, so ghostly the appearance of a vast black living shadow rising from the blue depths under the boat, and so queer the formation of the head in some, that they are universally known as Devil fish. And for all their harmless diet and their warning colour which considerately advises that one interferes with them at one's own risk, I join in hearty approval of their opprobrious name.

As is so sadly true of most marine organisms, we know far too little of their habits. What is the reason for the strange leaps they make into the air, falling back on to the water with a thudding splash that can be heard a mile away? It is usually done by night, a circumstance that adds to the strangeness of this sudden obtrusion upon our minds of the existence of a scarcely known world beneath the water, which we, in our preoccupation with our own half of the world, had almost forgotten.

So much for the prey, now to its hunting. They occasionally appear on the surface, two or three pairs swimming together, the black point of the side fin appearing above water, now on this side, now on that. On one occasion I was out in a small sailing boat with three or four canoes of pearl-divers, and as the fish when chased went down wind, we were able to follow, spread out in a long line so that whichever vessel saw the prey could signal to the others. We thus kept the chase going for an hour or more, striking with fish spears repeatedly, but as these are not barbed, and

[1] Unlike the Ballistes, some species at least are able to swallow the flesh of shellfish without the shells, so that the only indications of the origin of their diet is by finding opercula and radulae among the half-digested mass. They also break up pearl oysters, leaving the ground strewn with the broken shells.

as in all that hundred or more square feet of body the brain and heart occupy but a few square inches, the spears may go through and through, and be withdrawn again when all the line has been run out, with no appreciable damage to the animal. So on this occasion we made no capture, but the hour's chase over this silver sea with glimpses of mystery beneath was a pleasure to remember.

Another chase, also without capture, was stranger still. I found a pearling canoe moving over the dead calm sea with no visible means of propulsion. On reaching them I found they had made fast to a fish and dared not play the line attached to the spear for fear of its breaking away. Looking down into the blue with a water glass one saw the dim shadow of one of those monsters, *Pristis* by name, half shark, half ray, in which the snout is prolonged into a beak, into the sides of which are set formidable teeth, an object frequently exposed for sale in curio shops as the sawfish's jaw. This was one of the largest species of the genus and must have been ten to twelve feet long without the toothed snout.

We seemed to be in a dilemma; hauling upon the line would almost certainly withdraw the spear before the fish would be near enough for further attack, and the canoe had already been drifting about for two hours or so. However I understood that there was some hope of capture if the beast could be induced to approach shallow water, though I was left to wait and see the bold plan which was in the natives' minds. By dint of careful manœuvring we at last approached a reef, when one of the sailors unrove the boat's rigging and made a running noose with which he actually dived to the bottom, braving the six feet of two-edged saw, to slip the noose over the monster's tail! I, watching in safety from above, saw one of the finest diving feats imaginable, the man with the noose swimming to and fro, following the slow beats of the gigantic tail, watching his opportunity. Alas, as might have been expected, the monster was startled, a sudden wriggle and he disappeared, carrying the spear with him.

CHAPTER VI

DAILY LIFE—WOMEN

THEORETICALLY the women are supposed not to shew their faces and to be hidden from the world, liable to divorce at the caprice of the husband, and to be their downtrodden mindless slaves. As a matter of fact so far from men having four legal wives and numerous concubines, practically every marriage is monogamous. A tribe of nomads cannot enclose their women within high walls, and as for veiling, the most that is done is to hold a corner of their robe over the mouth, or perhaps between their teeth, and this is probably done as much to ward off the evil eye as from any ideas of modesty. No woman will, however, enter the yard enclosing my work-shops without urgent cause, and if brought into my office by her husband she covers her face completely and squats out of sight behind my writing table, whence the husband must cuff her on to her feet before business can proceed.

As a general rule the manner and look of the women is as of persons who know they have rights and a position, and who habitually make themselves heard in the family councils. Often I have been aware of the idea in a man's mind which in English might be expressed by "I must ask the Missis," and often it is bluntly put into words. Indeed, among these Northern tribes the women have a remarkable freedom, too much for the characters of many of them, as some subsequent anecdotes shew.

In any dispute brought before me, formally or informally, I find that, though it appears to be between men only, and to deal with men's concerns exclusively, a woman turns up sooner or later, and often that complainant's whole case has been put into his mouth by his wife or some female relative. It is safe to say that if the men only went to law on their own account, and were left to settle things their own way, the hard lot of the magistrate would be much lightened. While blaming the women, it is only fair to say that the men shew themselves born lawyers in their statements of a case. The complainant's account of a transaction makes things look black for the defendant, and certainly justifies his being sent for, even if a hundred miles away, but on his arrival one frequently finds that, though containing no direct lies, the complainant's story will bear a different interpretation.

As for divorce, and the consequent laxity of the marriage tie, all natives feel the difference between a regular marriage and an irregular alliance, and, if an individual did not, the wife's father and brothers would soon point it out. Indeed, a wife can keep her husband in due subjection by appeals to her relatives.

One morning, after we had been out at sea since sunrise, when I gave the signal for breakfast, one of my sailors remarked, "That is good news ; we *are* hungry this morning."

"Why more than usual ?"

"We were out with you yesterday till seven o'clock so when we got home there was no supper."

"But you are married men ; did not your wives have anything ready for you ?"

"Oh no, they had eaten their own suppers and gone to sleep. Women do as they like with us. You see, in a town we could go out and buy something ready cooked, but that is not possible here."

The idea that wifely duty involved getting up and providing something, rather than that a husband who had been kept at sea overtime should go hungry to bed, seemed to them a sweet, but unattainable ideal. I deprecate wife-beating, but I asked "Did you not feel inclined to strike them ?" but

Plate XXII

Fig. 48. Spinning goats' hair. Note nose ring and bead ornaments
(N.B. The word WAR on the tent door merely means that the sack
originally contained War Office stores)

that course would have meant settling with the father and brothers-in-law, the explanation that the husbands had come in hungry from the sea and had found no supper provided being, to their ideas, adequately met by the retort, "You must let them do as they like, that is the custom of our tribe and you must do as others do."

Marriage is by purchase, and though the bride has no choice, brothers and sons-in-law are carefully chosen. I once ventured on the impertinent question, "Now that your sister's marriage with so-and-so is not to take place who will she marry?"

"It is so hard to find a husband who will treat her well."

"Oh yes, of course you don't want her to marry a man who might beat her."

"No I don't, for if he did it would be my business to beat him, and I do not intend to have that bother put upon me," brotherly love being thus seen to have a practical side.

I know of few cases of legal polygamy and but one or two of concubinage. One of the former cases is that of my oldest skipper, a really good old man, whose one grief is that he remains childless near the close of life.

Divorce was suggested in a case of persistent causeless desertion, but the husband's reply was, " I took her when she was such a little thing, so I love her."

In another case the woman is a hopeless imbecile. Relatives begged me to fire a gun close to her head in the hope of awaking her senses, which I declared useless and dangerous, and refused to do. "She is my cousin, so I cannot divorce her," said the husband, an elderly man who shews her every kindness.

After some months of consultations, in which I shared and tried to act as peacemaker, one case actually did lead to divorce, and the lady was known as "the mother of Ali's child" instead of as Ali's wife. In a few weeks, however, Ali came begging for advance of wages. This being refused he entered into explanations, "You see I am going to take

my wife back. Being divorced, she has had nothing to eat
for a month, so now I must give her a good feed." This
literal translation of his speech must evidently be taken in the
spirit, for the lady still lives.

Pecuniary questions are so intimately associated with all
matters of marriage and divorce that men's actions must not
be read as though they indicated feelings only. In the same
way the women's independence is not only due to their knowledge of their value as women but also to the fact that the
husband, if of the poorer class, paid, say, six goats, a camel,
and four pounds in cash for them, besides providing for the
wedding feast, this involving a debt which will take him a
year or two to pay off, sometimes many years.

Ibrahim's story is a good illustration of the freedom of
women, which is often abused, and the subjection in which
they keep their men folk. It gives an instance also of the
pagan devil worship which is the real belief of these Muslim
when faced by calamity.

Ibrahim is a simple kindly old man, one of four brothers,
all of whom have passed their lives upon the sea. They are
old men now, and their sons are sailors too. The portrait
of one of the four is on Plate X, and decrepit though
he looks he still goes to sea in his own boat, or rather
canoe, taking the few goats which are his wealth across to an
island where a shower has fallen. There was a touch of
heroism when he came to me saying, "If you will give me
work as a sailor you will see I am quite strong still. I used
to be captain, but I cannot be that now as my eyes have gone
dim, but try me as a sailor."

Coming of such a family Ibrahim easily obtained the post
of skipper of my little schooner when it became vacant in my
absence. But though conscientious according to his lights,
and a good sailor in native fashion, he turned out to be not
quite the man we needed. He would travel two hundred
miles to fetch the letters, the arrival of which made a gleam
in the darkness of isolation in which we live here. His

arrival was the event of the month—or should have been, but his reply to the demand was often "Letters? I forgot." People who have never been quite alone for even one month cannot imagine the disappointment, though they may gauge the effect upon business.

As is so often the case here he was an elderly man when he married a girl of fourteen or less.

I once asked, "Do you think it really quite right for a white-haired old man to take a little girl like that?"

"If he has the money of course it is quite right" was the expected reply.

Marital love seems almost unknown, but family affection sometimes rises strong in later years, apart from its normal origin in the mutual love of young man and maid, but if the marriage is childless, or circumstances make it uncomfortable, the worst results follow in many cases.

His young wife, as wives often do here, one day decided that to live with her father's people in the hills would be more agreeable than with her husband by the sea. By and by Ibrahim began begging for leave to go to see her, his appeals that she should return to him having been in vain.

Her replies, as he repeated them to me, were certainly explicit. "I have only got a couple of girls by you. That's no good, so I don't want *you* any more."

Cases like this give rise to an immense amount of solemn conference between relatives to the nth degree and the village elders[1], in spite of the fact that many women go their own way in any case. The stages were reported to me at intervals, and in the end the woman reappeared of her own accord. Alas, her motive soon became obvious, for she was illegitimately "burdened," i.e. pregnant. So poor Ibrahim's joy was turned to anger and perplexity. He dearly loved his two little daughters, the two who were held as "not good

[1] The rather majestic term "Shêkh" often means nothing more than this, though it also includes persons of real importance and power in the country, and saints devoutly venerated.

enough" by their mother, and wished to keep them while divorcing the mother. My advice being asked (though I am about half the age of complainant) I was in a quandary, since the infants were not old enough to do without a woman's care and Ibrahim was not prepared with a substitute.

At this point I came home on leave, and on my return three months later I found that Ibrahim had actually become reconciled to his faithless wife; the child of "some young fellow in the hills" had been born a week or so, and the old man rejoiced over him as though he had been his own son.

A week later, and surely the hand of Providence was visible even to fatalists.

"Please come and see Ibrahim's wife, she is very ill." Even I could see that the woman was dying, and that nothing could be done for her, but at least I succeeded in saving the child from being fed on "samin," stinking native butter, which might soon have killed him.

The inconceivable stagnation of life in a desert coast village makes any event a godsend. Illness brings joy to all, even the sufferer seeming to be supported by the knowledge that he is a benefactor to the public. He is invariably surrounded by a deeply interested crowd, and never fails to shew appropriate symptoms.

In case of wounds the men are absolutely stoical, where a white man could not restrain evidence of suffering, and the application of a red hot nail, which is a frequent treatment for most complaints, is borne without a murmur. And so the gentle groaning of the sick is never allowed to become indecorous, but merely serves to prove that the host and patient is conscious of, and means to fulfil, his duty to his guests.

In this case things were very different, the woman was beyond even involuntary groans. The first thing to do was to send a boat for Ibrahim, who was absent on an island ten miles away. His return was delayed a full day by his going another five miles down the coast to the next village, where he spent a month's wages on new clothes and borrowed all the jewellery he could. With these his dying wife was decked out, as a means of persuading the evil spirit, which had caused her illness, to depart. At home meanwhile drums were being vigorously beaten outside the tent, a few feet away from her unconscious head, in the hope that what suasion could not effect in the mind of the malignant spirit might result from fear.

A stifling crowd of women and children filled the tiny tent, crowding upon the dying, while behind, in the shade, another party were making tea very cosily, around one who appeared to be already sewing the shroud.

The day after Ibrahim arrived the shrieks of this crowd of women suddenly announced the death. Within half an hour the body was buried and the mourners were about their ordinary occupations. Ibrahim wept like a child, though why he should grieve for such a wife it is hard for a white man to say.

Negro women, being escaped or liberated slaves, and so having no relatives who can settle disputes with their husbands, sometimes come in to complain of being beaten, though they owe protection to the fact that negro women are fewer than the men, so that a husband who is disagreeable to his wife runs the risk of losing that valuable property. Hamitic women only come to try and get an increased allowance from their husbands rarely to complain of ill-treatment, from which they are protected by their relatives.

The making and mending of clothes, that great part of women's daily work, is non-existent with us, for, as before stated, the lengths of flimsy cotton are worn as they come from the shop. Washing is often in progress, rather a miserable business in sea-water without soap, but the thinness of the stuff makes it easier[1].

---

[1] Donkeys' dung provides a cheap substitute for soap. The clothes are buried in the sand of the sea-shore with dung, left overnight and washed out in the sea next day.

Besides cooking and the care of children and animals the women have certain manufactures. The palm-leaf matting for the outer covering of the tents and houses is bought ready made, but the inner coarse blanket material is woven at home from the hair of the owner's goats, which is collected and spun into coarse thread as it becomes available. The spinning is entirely by hand, the thread being merely wound on a dangling stick which is kept spinning by hand. When a dozen or so large balls of this grey-black and brown thread have accumulated, a rough weaving frame of three sticks is pegged out on the sand, and weaving goes on for some days. Neighbours are called in to help, three to six women generally working together.

Any man passing near women who are working at blanket making must beware lest they should throw the balls of wool at him. If he is struck by one the women have the right to demand a present, which is divided among the helpers.

The palm-leaves used in basket making and for the "Serîr" or sleeping mat are brought from Suakin, no palms growing in all our country. These baskets are so closely woven that when once the fibres are thoroughly wetted they become watertight. The figures on Plate XVI illustrate a milk-bowl made in this way; the other baskets have covers and are used to keep women's trinkets &c., or the fragile earthenware coffee-pot, one being ornamented by the interweaving of strips of thin leather, the other by pieces of red flannel and tufts of camels' hair. In other cases the leaves are bought ready dyed and the resulting basket displays bands of colour.

In making a "Serîr," or sleeping mat, a woman slits up the midribs of palm leaves and provides a number of goat-skins scraped free of hair. These skins are cut into narrow strips like string and woven in and out between the palm midribs which are laid side by side, and the number of skins used in making one mat is surprising. The work is tedious,

Plate XXIII

Fig. 49. Weaving. Behind the three women is finished blanket, in front the threads of the warp

Fig. 50. Marriageable girl of thirteen cooking rice in antique brass pot

and she gets neighbours' help ; the result, as an addition to comfort, seems hardly worth the labour.

It is the women's business to strike and pitch the tents. In the village this is done not only on arrival and departure, but after the tent has stood some time in one place it is shifted to a fresh site by way of a "spring cleaning."

Old women and children drive the goats out to "graze" in the desert in the early morning and may feed and tether them on their return, but, as already remarked in Chapter III, a peculiar superstition declares that men must do the milking. They also bring water from the well, in goat-skins on donkeys.

Women suffer sometimes from a mysterious disease, the symptoms of which seem closely to resemble those of the "vapours" of our ancestresses. The help of a female shêkh has to be called in, sometimes at great expense. First seeing the patient she prescribes what articles of clothing, especially what ornaments, are to be worn, and then goes off alone into the desert, where, according to my informant, she behaves like a maniac, apparently invoking good and exorcising evil spirits. "Vapours" would of course yield most easily to suggestion, and the little break in the monotony of life, the fuss and mild excitement, are quite enough to bring about a cure.

In my demonstration of the independence of women even in a Moslem community I am conscious that the less agreeable side of their character becomes unduly prominent. I would now leave on record that in many cases the standard of wifely duty is far above what one has any right to expect from the conditions of their lives.

The best women are often the least conspicuous members of any community, but their presence is made evident in the existence of any kind of prosperity or real happiness. I conclude my account by saying that in this village amid all the laxity of an Oriental civilisation bordering on savagery, in spite of its desolation and poverty, lack of defence against

c.

6

either the dreadful heat of summer or the cold of winter, the hunger that makes men eat the food of cattle, and where fresh water is often an unattainable luxury, men find the happiness of home in a way which multitudes of our own urban poor do not know. Where this is so goodness must necessarily be ; though its laws differ from those we ourselves know, its presence is none the less evident.

Plate XXIV

Fig. 51. Baby girl with lamb, which is *not* woolly

PART II

CHAPTER VII

CORALS AND CORAL ANIMALS

DIRECTLY we look at the ground in the neighbourhood of Port Sudan or Suakin, or indeed anywhere on this part of the Red Sea coast, we see that it is largely composed of shells and fragments of coral. Further, it is easy to see that these differ from the fossils of home limestones in their extreme abundance. in their lying loose among the surrounding sand, and in their being familiar to the collector of shells as common species still living in the neighbouring sea. The same is true of the corals, though in this case the identification is not quite so obvious. The fact is we are walking upon a coral-reef, almost exactly like those still forming and growing in the sea, which has been elevated by earth movements above the water, and every grain of the earth was once part of a living creature.

Such elevated coral-reefs are common in the world, but they rarely remain so little altered by the upheaval as here. All this dry land and these splendid harbours, many mountain masses in different parts of the world, innumerable islands in the Pacific and Indian Oceans rising from enormous depths of water, are monuments of the life-activity of certain lowly organisms.

So much is generally understood, but too often the vision is of "patient insects building islands in the deep." At least the visitor to the new town of Port Sudan must recognise the coral organism as the fundamental fact of all that he has

Fig. 52. A simple sea-anemone.

Figs. 53 and 54. Young and fully developed colonial anemones.

Figs. 55 and 56. Two views of a living coral polyp (*Caryophyllia smithii*) from above and from the side. The radial plates of limestone, conspicuous in Fig. 57, are seen through the transparent body wall. Otherwise the animal is like Fig. 52.

(Drawn from living animal by H. C. Chadwick, A.L.S.)

Fig. 57. The stony cup of *Caryophyllia*, seen from above and from the side, after removal of the polyp's flesh.

Plate XXV

Fig. 52

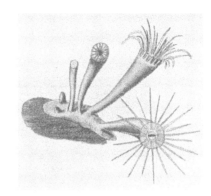

Fig. 53

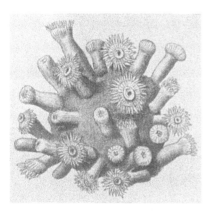

Fig. 54

Fig. 55

Fig. 56

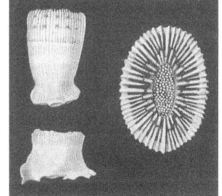

Fig. 57

Sea-anemones and corals

come so far to see. They are the builders of those foundations of which the great quay-walls are but a trimming and straightening of an infinitesimal portion, but it is no more possible to directly observe the building action of the coral polyps than to see the growth of the bones in a child.

An examination of any typical coral fragment, living or dead, massive or branched, shews that the surface of the stone is shaped into little cups, which may be large (half an inch or more in diameter) or very small; they may entirely cover the surface or be scattered at intervals, be sunk below the general level or project boldly from it (see the figures of corals on Plate XXVI). In any case, all ordinary corals consist of a multitude of such cups borne upon a common mass of the same stony material, and each cup may be regarded as the remains of one individual "polyp" as the coral animal is called.

It will be a simpler way of gaining an idea of what a coral polyp really is to take a least specialised member of its class, one in which each individual lives disconnected from its fellows and does not secrete the complicated skeleton characteristic of the stony corals. Fig. 52 shews a "sea-anemone" in no material respect different to those which Gosse has so beautifully figured from our own shores. It is seen to be a graceful translucent cylinder fixed by its base to some chance stone or shell. This extreme simplicity of form gives the living animal a by no means inconsiderable beauty.

The free end of the cylinder bears a circle of what look like hairs, but which are found on testing to be highly sensitive to touch and are surprisingly adhesive for organs of such transparent delicacy. They are consequently better named the tentacles, their function being to adhere to and close down upon any little water-flea or such-like animal that has the bad luck to swim against them. They are also provided with stinging cells which are used for paralysing their prey and for defence. In the centre of the disc is the mouth, a simple opening, a mere hole in the top of a sac.

Our polyp, or anemone, has no organs of locomotion, no organs of sight, taste or hearing, indeed no brain. It has at any rate the rudiments of a nervous and muscular system, for it is able to move its tentacles all towards that one which has captured prey and assist it in conveying the food to the mouth. The body is sensitive all over, for any part when touched will contract, and a violent shock causes the tentacles to fold together and the whole animal to close down to a shapeless hemispherical mass. This is the limit of its sensory and muscular powers, two or three muscular movements, a few of the simplest reactions to outside influences, nothing that could be called even the *sense* of touch.

Internally again the principal interest of the organism is its extreme simplicity. There is no stomach or gut, no heart or veins, no lung or gills, no kidneys and no brain. The animal is in fact a simple sac, the inner walls are much folded to increase their area, but there is but one body-space to serve for everything. In this space the food is digested. There is but one opening into it from the outside, so the indigestible remnants of the food are voided by the same opening as that they entered by.

Simplicity of organisation could scarcely go farther; we have here an example of one of the lowest forms of life. Lowly organisms of this kind shew an astonishing indifference to the separation of one part from another. No cutting or mutilation does any permanent harm. Chop the beast to fragments, and not only will each piece remain alive, but it will grow until it encloses a new sac, forms a new mouth, tentacles, and adhesive base, and behold a number of new and complete polyps. This possibility has been taken advantage of by nature, and numbers of these lowly forms of life propagate themselves in this way. A projection arises on the side of the animal, is automatically amputated, grows missing organs, and becomes a complete and independent animal. The process is exactly like the planting of rose-cuttings, one of the cases of asexual reproduction in the animal kingdom.

Now in many cases, where propagation by buds takes place, the buds undergo their full development into complete polyps while remaining connected with the parent. An example of a "colony" of sea-anemones thus formed is given by Plate XXV, Figs. 53 and 54. An allied form, known as *Palythoa*, is common in the Red Sea as little star-like rings of tentacles, of a beautiful deep, yet bright, green, carpeting the sand and stones in shallow water. Each star, or polyp head, measures about a quarter-inch in diameter, so that when a few dozen occur together they form a quite conspicuous patch of colour.

As already stated the corals are similar "colonial" organisms, the numerous cups on their stony branches representing each one polyp head. But how the polyps are connected with the stony material is best explained by, as before, taking the simplest possible case, that of a solitary non-colonial polyp, which is exactly like our simple sea-anemone, but has a stony cup like one of those of the ordinary corals.

Plate XXV, Figs. 55 and 56, represents such a form, which is in fact the only British stony coral[1]. But for differences in shape and proportion, the upper part of the organism is exactly similar to the sea-anemone shewn in Fig. 52, but beneath it is a stony mass, the coral cup, secreted by the base of the polyp, a seat exactly adapted to its own shape. The empty cup, after removal of the anemone, is shewn as seen from above in Fig. 57, to the right, and the curious radial plates of the same stony matter, so characteristic of all coral cups, are very plain. This polyp is comparatively large, measuring half an inch or more across.

This cup is not formed in the complicated way in which bone is made in the higher animals. The material is the cheapest possible, viz. limestone; this occurs in minute quantities in solution in all sea-water, and the coral polyp has

---

[1] Except certain rare forms obtainable only from very deep water in the Atlantic.

Seriatopora

Galaxea   Favia

Porites   Coeloria   Stylophora
(another form)

Siderastrea   Favia

                    Pavonia

Pavonia   Pocillopora

Pocillopora   Porites   Hydniopora
                 (a common kind)

Plate XXVI

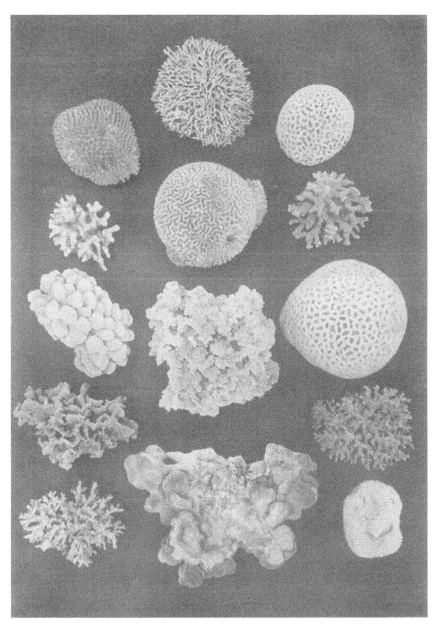

Fig. 58. Stony corals of 13 species belonging to 9 genera;
generic names only given

Plate XXVII

Fig. 59. *Dendrophyllia*, a simple colonial coral with distinct polyp cups

the power of absorbing it[1] from the water and rendering it insoluble and stony in just those places where it is needed to form the kind of cup characteristic of the species. Another difference from bone is that the secretion is altogether outside the body of the animal; the cup is a mere dead structure from the first. One can imagine the animal as throwing down a limestone seat for itself, and as the seat thickens the polyp is raised more and more above the sea-bottom.

Imagine now the polyp to bud, as does *Palythoa*, and each bud to secrete its own cup, while the connecting branches also throw down the same limestone, so that the cups are connected on to one mass, and we have at once the formation of ordinary reef coral, of which perhaps the simplest possible case is the *Dendrophyllia*, figured on Plate XXVII, where each polyp gives rise to but one bud, which gives out one other, so each branch is like a simple chain of polyps and their cups. The other corals figured are rather more complicated, since one polyp gives off many buds, and their branches are correspondingly more massive. In the hemispherical corals, the connecting branches are short, practically non-existent, and the polyps are crowded together, as a kind of skin, over the solid mass of limestone they have secreted. Certain species of coral form enormous colonies, containing hundreds of thousands of little polyps. I remember a certain part of the fringing reef of Zanzibar[2] over which the water was 6 feet or more deep. Being perfectly clear, and so favourable to coral growth, it was inhabited by a species of the genus *Porites*, which formed huge cylinders, the flat tops measuring 6 to 12 feet across, level with that of the lowest spring-tide, since it is impossible for the polyps to live above that level. So closely were these great cylinders planted in the water that it was easy,

---

[1] More correctly by decomposition of calcium sulphate, thus,

$$CaSO_4 + H_2CO_3 = CaCO_3 + H_2SO_4,$$

since the sulphate forms $3\cdot6\,\%$ while the carbonate only forms $0\cdot2\,\%$ of the salts dissolved in sea-water.

[2] Similar masses are common in the Red Sea, but I do not know of a case quite so striking as this.

by striding and jumping from one to another, to cross the channel to the shallower part of the reef on the other side.

From what has been said of the formation of the coral cups it is clear that the quantity of living matter going to the formation of these great cylinders is very small, a mere gelatinous film over the surface.

The fundamental simplicity of structure, which is common to every coral, does not preclude the evolution of an amazing variety of forms. In the course of time as many species have been evolved as there are possible combinations of the conditions, animate and inanimate, which affect coral growth and survival. In form these range from huge and solid stones, weighing many tons, to tiny delicate things like petrified lace or ferns, some of substance nearly as hard as shells, others so spongy as to be easily cut into by a knife. I have been enabled to give two plates illustrating a few out of this amazing variety. Both massive, hemispherical or dome-shaped, and more delicate branched species are shewn, but lobed growths, such as that shewn at the bottom of the first group, intergrade the two divisions. The latter specimen is of particular interest, being a species of the genus *Porites*, already referred to as forming great cylinders of solid stone. This small specimen was taken from shallow water, near lowest tide level, so that the polyp cups, which are too small to be visible in the photograph, were intact only on its sides. Above they were killed by the air and sun, and the stone they had formed, being exposed to the action of the sea, has been dissolved away slightly, leaving a narrow rim round the edge, where the part that was protected by living flesh shews the height the colony originally attained.

In the middle of the plate are small dome-shaped colonies, of species which, though rarely growing to the size of the *Porites* cylinders, may form very considerable boulders. Notice the different shapes of the polyp cups, with their radiating plates, and the varying beauty they impart to the

Plate XXVIII

Fig. 60. Stony corals
All are forms of genus *Madrepora* except the lowest, which is
a species of *Symphyllia*

surface of the stone, a beauty which is enhanced by examination under a lens.

Most of the branched kinds belong to one great genus *Madrepora*, one of the most conspicuous of all the forms seen in a living reef, and which contains a very great number of species. In spite of the wide variety of outer shape, the structure of the coral polyps is almost identical throughout this genus. The colonies may be quite small and are generally of moderate size, but one tremendous growth has been recorded, which covered an acre of the sea bottom and sent its branches of stone to the height of 50 feet. In this case a single coral equalled in size a plantation of large trees, but what is usually seen is a network of branches springing from one thick stem and spreading horizontally, and covering a fan-shaped or circular area of a square yard at most.

Not only are the growth-forms of corals varied as those of plants, but the details of the polyp cups are well worth attention. Typically the surface of the coral is covered with round depressions, which may be minute, as in *Porites*, or half an inch across as in *Caryophyllia* and the dome-shaped species shewn on Plate XXVI. All are partially filled up by complicated series of radial plates, and a central core, best seen in the illustration of *Caryophyllia*, and the arrangement and ornamentation of these form an endless variety of patterns. In other cases the depressions, instead of being round, are elongated, forming meandering grooves over the surface, which, from their superficial likeness to the convolutions of the human brain, give the name "Brain coral" to certain kinds. In others again the walls of the cups disappear, and the system is reduced to a network of plates, converging to the centres of the polyps, or these may be so thickened and flattened that the spaces between them appear as fine lines, tracing a lace-like pattern on the surface of the stone.

One is tempted to write a whole book on the beauties of corals and coral animals but must refrain : one other form is however so interesting, and at the same time so common, that a short special description is given.

In many sheltered water gardens may be seen numbers of what look like overturned, stalkless, mushrooms. On handling they are found to lie loose on the sand and to be stony corals. They are in fact single polyps of phenomenal size, being up to six inches across, and the radiating plates, which so resemble the "gills" of a mushroom (hence the name of this genus, *Fungia*) correspond to those already seen in the other corals illustrated. The cup wall is however absent.

The life history is as strange as the coral that results. The young polyp produces at first a quite ordinary, small, cylindrical cup, Plate XXIX, which is fixed to a stone in the usual way. After reaching a certain size this swells at the top into a disc, like a mushroom on its stalk, except that the mushroom head is turned wrong side up. A little later this head falls off on to the sand, where it continues to grow into the big *Fungia* discs first met with. This, however, is not the death of the original polyp, which goes on growing new heads which in turn fall off, *ad infinitum*!

Many attempts have been made to visualise the beauties of a coral garden, in poetry, romance, and works of sober science. I can make no claim for my own picture, but that perhaps it is written with better acquaintance than is generally possible to poets and romanticists, and that it is free from exaggeration, as the writings of a biologist should be.

Let us imagine our exploration from the beginning. It is a calm morning in summer, the sea a pearl of beauty, under the new-risen sun. The heat, great even in the early morning, is unnoticed in enjoyment of the delicate pink and blue and golden shades reflected by the mirror-like surface, unbroken by any indication of what lies below. The tints of reef and shoal, which form so beautiful a part of the seascape when the water is rippled, are now exchanged for atmospheric colours, which, as we float over from deep to shallow water, give place to a panorama of coral gardens below.

Plate XXIX

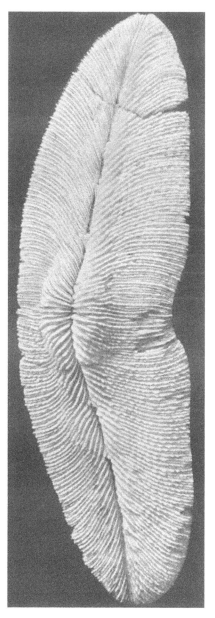

Fig. 62

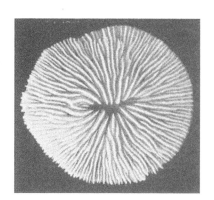

Fig. 61   Fig. 63

Mushroom Corals

Fig. 61. *Herpolitha*, an elongated fungid
Fig. 62. The young form of *Fungia*
Fig. 63. A typical *Fungia*-disc

As we row, keeping watch ahead, the reef seems suddenly to spring up before us, so steep is its slope.

The pleasure of the sight of a new and beautiful world of shapes and colours, mimicking yet utterly unlike those of life on land, is for us enhanced by the vigour of its life and growth, in happy contrast to the desert shore.

On the edge of the shoal *Porites* and other solid forms appear as great rocky buttresses among the lighter plant-like growths, or, a little way from it may rise from the depths as an isolated pillar. In many places in the Red Sea such coral pinnacles abound in comparatively deep water, a horror of unexpected danger to the sailor.

There is nothing more fascinating than the edge of a reef in the open sea, where numbers of forms and their delightful groupings can be seen in succession, one below another, till they become hazy and gradually lost in the blue depths, sixty to ninety feet below us. There are precipices clothed with a thick bush of spreading coral, some seeking the light by reaching out horizontally, others by growing upwards tree fashion, what appear to be bare rocks turning out to be massive colonies, as much alive as the more plant-like forms, caves, dark in contrast to the bright corals that surround their mouths, and the white shell-sand with which they are floored.

The general colour of living corals is very various, the snow white or creamy skeletons seen in museums being covered by a tinted film of polyps. The majority of species are some shade of brown, from deep chocolate to the golden colour of some seaweed covered boulders on home shores, but among these bright tints are abundant. The brown branches of *Madrepora* are generally tipped with light violet, pink or white, as though each ended in a flower, while other branched corals are a brilliant scarlet or bright green all over. Another forms a series of large thin sheets, spreading horizontally one above another, and all of a brilliant yellow! In these the flesh is inconspicuous, appearing as a mere colouring of the stony branches, but in others the polyps are as conspicuous as "sea-anemones," with typical flower-like discs, a row of tentacles surrounding the mouth, or the tentacles may be so long that nothing else is visible. One of these, *Galaxea*, is very beautiful, shades of bright or dark green mingling with a greater or less proportion of brown, so that the rounded knolls of coral may resemble hillocks of grass, or of brown seaweed. Another large coral is almost devoid of tentacles altogether, but the polyps are large and the stone is covered as it were with green brown velvet, laid down in soft folds.

Of the inhabitants of these gardens and grottoes there is no space to speak. Anemones of all sizes and colours abound, and flower-like animals, the most beautiful of which are the sensitive sea-worms, add colour even to the corals. The gorgeous fish that lazily pass in and out, as though flaunting their beauty they could be careless of danger, have been described by every traveller.

The association between certain smaller fish, crabs and other higher animals with corals is remarkable. One sees for instance a branched coral with a shoal of tiny green fish hovering near, or in another case the fish are banded vertically black and white. Drop a pebble among them and they instantly disappear among the branches, and if the coral is taken out of the water the fish still cling to their refuge, and most of them are captured with it. These are but two examples of a whole world of life found only among corals.

Seeing that all corals are derivable from the sea-anemone (some form of which must have been the original ancestor of the whole family), and that the sea-anemone has been proved to be very distinctly an animal, I trust that the animal nature of the corals is now too firmly fixed in the reader's mind to be shaken by their vegetable fixity, vegetative growth and form, or even by the fact that I am about to explain, viz. that the majority of corals do *not* obtain their nourishment by the capture of prey, but by the decomposition of the carbonic acid gas contained in the sea-water, a method of feeding which is the most distinctive feature of plant-life as opposed to animal. To recapitulate the well-known and fundamental fact of the life of this world, the plants are characterised by their taking up carbonic acid gas which, by the power of sunlight upon their green matter, they split up in some way so as to form starch from the carbon with water, while the oxygen is liberated back into the air. The animals, on the other hand, eat the food ready prepared for them by the plants, which is consumed in their bodies, and burned, as it were, back to carbonic acid, which land-animals get rid of in breathing. So there is a balance, the oxygen necessary to animal life being freed by the plants from the carbonic acid given by the animals, which carbonic acid is the necessary food-stuff of the plants.

The process in the sea is exactly similar, only that the gases concerned are dissolved in the water and rarely separate and become visible as bubbles. Fishes give off carbonic acid gas, dissolved in the sea-water, from their gills, and this is broken up by the seaweeds which liberate the oxygen from which the fishes and all animals re-form carbonic acid gas.

Now the amazing thing about the corals is that the polyps have entered into an alliance with certain microscopic plants which come to live in their bodies, and they feed upon the starchy products these plants form in sunlight, and even upon the plants themselves. So intimate is the union of these strange partners that neither can live without the other, the coral has lost its independence, and in fact as well as in appearance leads the life of a plant. At the first sight of a coral sea one wonders what takes the place of the great beds of brown and green weed which fringe British shores, and are a source of the oxygen essential to animal life. The discovery of these plant partners of the corals gives the answer. This easy life, this evasion of the necessity of capturing prey, is doubtless the reason for the degeneration of the polyp structure noticed above.

One of the greatest interests of these lowly forms of life is their place in the evolution of the higher. We have left all that is familiar, the creatures with heads and limbs, far behind, on the surface as it were, and are groping among the foundations of the edifice of creation. It is difficult indeed to express how very far down we are without some description of the rest of the series. But this is impossible; I am asked to give means of understanding what a coral is, and should not be thanked for giving in reply a treatise on Zoology. Let us take two steps only of the process of evolution, and let these short lengths give an expression of the whole descent.

Consider the vast interval of time and changes of structure involved in the evolution of man from his ape-like ancestor. How many thousands of years, what vast advances! How far above the purely animal is the lowest savage, and how far above that the best of civilised man! And yet even in the case of the brain, the development of which is man's main advance, the man's brain is but the further development of the ape's[1], which has already gone the greater part of the way manwards from the condition found in ordinary animals.

Now we and the apes together are derived from some fish-like ancestor. We all had gill bars fundamentally like those of a fish at one stage of our existences. It is a vast descent through the reptiles to the amphibia and then to the fishes[2]! And the fishes again are our second step illustrative of the vast changes involved. Fish are just fish to the ordinary man, and yet the fact is that the difference between man and ape is just nothing to that between the ordinary higher fish, the kinds that come in after the soup, and the

[1] The apes include a wide variety of type, e.g. the baboon is on the whole lower than the ordinary monkey, which is lower than the big man-like apes, chimpanzee, orang-outang and gorilla. The lemurs link lower monkeys and ordinary quadrupeds. See Huxley's essay "On the relations of man to the lower animals," 1863.

[2] Avoid the conception of descent as the highest fish giving rise to the lowest amphibian, the highest amphibian giving birth to the lowest reptile, and so on. The fishes did not cease their evolution when the amphibia appeared, and ancestral types must have been generalised, and so, in one sense, lowly forms.

sharks. The shark family have not yet attained the possession of true bone, for instance, and their brain development is almost rudimentary. But we are already in the dim beginnings of geological history, for sharks essentially like those we now know were living when almost the earliest of rocks were being laid down as mud in primeval oceans. These were times incredibly remote, when land animals were not in existence, when plants were represented only by seaweeds, the whole land a desert but for possibly some creeping films of vegetation adapted to life on damp soil ashore, times long ages before those strange reptiles Iguanodon, Diplodocus, the whale-like Ichthyosaurus, the giant ferns and lycopods of the coal measures, whose fossil remains remind us of nightmare worlds which have passed away, had ever come into being.

We are at the beginning of geological history, and yet the corals are a large and flourishing class, coral-reefs are growing as nowadays, and the corals themselves, though of course of altogether different forms, are essentially the same down to the first syllable of recorded time. But having proofs of evolution which are independent of the geological record over these vast aeons, we may safely carry back the process into those times represented by rocks so ancient that no fossil trace of life is found in them, to the times when the lowest fish-like vertebrata were not, and the simple polyp was the highest product of life upon the earth. We know that most probably there really was such a time, but to imagine it is like trying to comprehend the solar system by arithmetic. We may speculate and wonder at the first beginnings of life, but I, for one, prefer to leave it to each reader's imagination.

CHAPTER VIII

THE BUILDING OF REEFS

SEA-WATER, besides containing comparatively large quantities of common salt, contains several other substances in solution in less quantity. One of these is the limestone[1] which the coral polyp extracts and renders solid as its stony skeleton, and of which, in essentially the same way, the "shell fish," whether oyster, winkles or crabs make their hard coverings. Another constituent is magnesium carbonate, a substance rather similar to limestone, to which we refer later.

Having examined the individual stone formed by the growth of a coral colony we must consider how such stones are aggregated to form a reef.

It is obvious that colonies cannot live for ever, any more than do individuals, and we need to know the fate of a dead colony and how it is replaced by a living one which shall continue the building. So great is the competition among the crowds of the floating young of the fixed animals that any vacant spot is at once appropriated. When a coral colony dies the coloured film of flesh speedily rots away and the snow-white stony skeleton remains, washed clean by waves and currents[2]. In a few days this is covered with a film of

[1] More accurately gypsum, $CaSO_4$, which is decomposed to form limestone $CaCO_3$ as noted bottom of page 89 above.

[2] To obtain a specimen of coral of this beautiful snow-white colour it is necessary to remove the flesh from any living colony, which is usually coloured brown or yellow, by rotting the same for a week in sea-water in a bucket. Cover the bucket to keep out dust, and change the water a few times to reduce the smell. The last traces of decayed flesh are removed by dashing buckets of water on to the coral. Rinse in fresh water. Or the specimens may be dried *thoroughly*, rotted in water after return to Europe, and finally bleached with hydrogen peroxide.

the finest green seaweed, invisible among which are the embryos of several orders of animals, e.g. shell-fish, or, there may be the larvae of some other coral. There is a tense struggle for survival among these young creatures, but on a growing reef conditions of course generally favour the coral's young (otherwise the reef would cease to grow), some of which grow at the expense of nearly everything else and cover the site. Many of the large hemispherical corals live on the reef like loose stones, but on turning them over one may find quite a small shell, or coral branch, attached to the centre of the underside. This is the foundation of the whole, the resting place of the tiny floating larva, the growth of which first covered the stone on which it settled by a vigorous colony which when large enough to be independent of support continued its growth until the mass exceeded by hundreds of times the bulk of the original foundation.

The more delicate of coral skeletons, such as those of the porous branched madrepores, rarely survive the death of the polyps that formed them. On losing its coat of living flesh the coral is exposed to the action of boring animals, as well as to the direct solvent action of the sea-water, and many are thus destroyed. Partly they go back into solution, but the greater portion is broken down to mud and sand. In shallow water branched colonies are broken up into pebbles and coarse sand by the waves, and these materials serve to fill in the spaces between the larger colonies and pack the whole together into a solid mass.

There are other constituents of coral reefs of not very much less importance than the corals themselves. Large masses are formed of the bivalve shells which live in the coral mud, and which, by the solidification of this mud, form with it a limestone, such as that of which the houses of Port Sudan are built. Although among the very numerous and conspicuous fossils of this stone coral branches are not the commonest, yet the mass of shells and hardened mud is every bit as much a part of the reef as anything else is. In some reefs too, even where coral is growing abundantly, the shells of the great clam *Tridacna* are so abundant as to make up a considerable part of the total mass. Others again contain quantities of certain peculiar seaweeds (of which the "coralline" of British seas is one) which, though true plants in every detail, have the property of taking up limestone from the sea and forming therewith a skeleton, even harder and more compact than that of the corals. Plate XXX shews the appearance of these plants, and will enable the reader to identify some of those he meets with. These sometimes form a cement, by which the coral colonies and fragments are held together, and in some others the whole reef is formed of them[1]. Other organisms assist, but I observe my principle of dealing only with the most important features and desist from enumerating all.

This is the whole structure of the interior of such a reef as that which fringes the Red Sea coast, as seen e.g. during the excavation of the quay walls or slipway at Port Sudan. Great "stones" which are the more massive colonies, generally the genus *Porites*, are bedded in with smaller colonies whole or broken. In places are collections of grey mud and sand, also formed from coral by the action of boring organisms or perhaps as the residue left after partial solution by the sea.

"How fast does a coral reef grow?" is a question often asked, and never as yet truly answered. Probably each of the hundreds of species of coral has its own maximum rate of growth, which is however rarely attained, as it is certain that the rate of every colony of each species varies very widely with its position on the reef and its immediate surroundings. So taking the rate of growth of a few samples would go a very little way towards giving that of the corals in any given

[1] See for instance, among other literature by the same author, "The Fauna and Geography of the Maldives and Laccadives," Cambridge University Press, and "The Percy Sladen Trust Expedition to the Indian Ocean," by J. Stanley Gardiner, M.A., F.R.S., etc., *Transactions Linnean Soc. Zoology*, Vol. XII., pp. 35, 51, and illustrations on Plate IX, and on pages 128 and 135.

Plate XXX

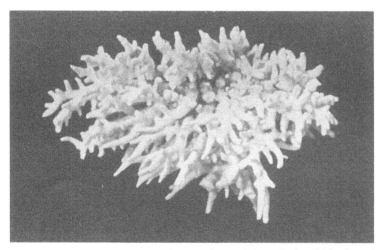

Figs. 64 and 65. Stony seaweeds, massive and branched. *Lithothamnia*

square yard of the reef edge. Although individual colonies may grow quite rapidly this is but half the question. We must know also full details of the action of eroding and transporting sea currents, solution, boring organisms (in coral, coral sand and mud) and subtract the total from that of the deposition of stone by living polyps, to obtain the net increase.

The boring animals mentioned as reducing coral stone to mud are very easily found and examined. Almost any old worn piece of coral, and many still living colonies, are found to be studded with small slit-like holes with slightly raised borders. On breaking into the stone each hole is found to lead at once into an oval cavity, say an inch long by three-eighths in diameter, containing a bivalve shell of about the same size, *Lithodomus* by name, from its appearance known as the "date shell," which has made the hollow and is continually enlarging it. Other colonies when broken across instead of shewing pure white limestone are found to be honeycombed with yellow or red spongy matter. This is the sponge *Clione*, which has the property, especially astonishing in a sponge, of boring into any limestone, whether coral or shell, making it quite rotten and so, finally, reducing it to mud and sand.

Certain worms live in the same way. The largest species of these, by name *Eunice siciliensis*, attains a length of a yard or so, and the thickness of a quarter of an inch, but so intricate is its boring that it is practically impossible to extract a full-grown specimen entire. The head end is at the innermost part of the burrow, and when extracted the two white gouge-like teeth, by which the burrow is cut out, are easily seen.

There is a fish too, *Pseudoscarus* by name, which actually lives on coral! It is commonly taken by fishermen and is easily recognised by its gorgeous green, blue and pink colours, but particularly by its teeth, which are fused into two pairs of chisels, with which the surface of the coral, and with it its

Figs. 66 and 67. Two specimens of *Porites*.

In 66 the flesh has been left on the coral and where it is broken it is seen that the dark coloured living matter penetrates the mass only to the bottoms of the coral cups. In this small piece the openings of 14 *Lithodomus* burrows are seen, and in four of them the lips of the shell are visible.

In 67 the base of the still living coral is rotting away, being full of small holes formed by the sponge *Clione* and small boring worms.

Fig. 68. An old piece of coral in which so much of the surface has rotted away that the numerous *Lithodomus* borings, of which only the small openings can be seen in living corals, are fully exposed. This in spite of partial protection by growth of encrusting stony seaweed as at the point marked *a*.

Fig. 69. Section of a large shell, a material very much harder than any coral, yet bored in the same way by both mollusca and sponge.

Fig. 70. The mollusc *Pholas* lying in its burrow in coral.

Fig. 70 about natural size, the rest about half this.

From specimens in the Cambridge University Museum of Zoology.

Plate XXXI

Fig. 66

Fig. 68

Fig. 67

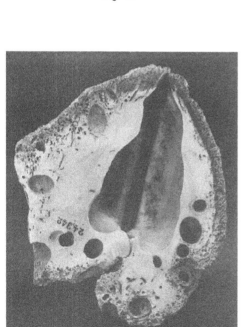

Fig. 69

Fig. 70

Borings of molluscs and sponges

living matter, is browsed away.   Cut open a specimen of this
fish and you find its guts full of fragments of coral[1].

Pholas, another boring bivalve mollusc, common in shales
on some British coasts, is less often seen.   Its burrow is
deeply buried in a solid living colony separated from the
outside by a comparatively long passage.   But it is not nearly
so common as the preceding forms, and lives more solitary,
Lithodomus generally occurring in numbers together.

After the coral has been broken down by these means,
the sand is further reduced to fine mud by the action of those
animals which live by burrowing in it, and passing large
quantities through their guts, after the manner of earth-
worms.   Just as there is a great fauna which lives on the
nourishment filtered from large quantities of sea-water[2] so
there is another great and varied community of sand eaters.
There are first of all the worms, next, but more important in
the tropics, great numbers of large holothurians or "sea
slugs" (though slugs they are *not*), some of which crawl on
and eat only the surface sand, but one species burrows deeply
and raises casts like an earthworm, but a hundred times the size.
Considering the large effects produced by the ordinary earthworm in a year, that resulting from the presence of animals
hundreds of times their bulk, whose casts in many lagoons
entirely cover the bottom, must be very considerable indeed.

One observation that can be made by anybody is to note
how long it is before corals reappear once a reef has been
cleared out, e.g. for the foundations of a quay wall.   Two
small portions of an apparently growing reef at Port Sudan
were buried under a pile of stones for the foundations of the
east and west Customs landings, and four years later there

---

[1] The duller coloured and peculiarly shaped "bladder" or "parrot" fish,
Tetraodon or "four tooth" is distinguished by its peculiarly rounded shape and
alteration of scales into spines.   Though its teeth are very similar to the coral
eater, *Pseudocarus*, it eats softer animals, e.g. Ascidians and Echinoderms, and
sometimes shell-fish.

[2] Includes the whole oyster and bivalve shell-fish family, and many other less
generally known forms of life.

was no growth of coral on the artificial slopes thus made, though every condition apparently remains as favourable as before. Again at a point inside Dongonab Bay, where coral growth is luxuriant in shallows, the coral was some years ago collected from one spot and a sea wall built with it. A few small colonies have established themselves upon the sides of the wall after an interval of twelve years ; they are perfectly healthy, yet their bulk is an infinitesimal fraction of that removed from the wall by solution and attrition. This shews how even among growing coral one cannot be sure that the degradation of rock to sand and mud is not in excess of aggradation, i.e. its building up by coral organisms, and how a lagoon may be rapidly eating away its encircling reefs and yet contain comparatively luxuriant coral gardens.

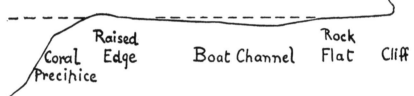

Diagram 1. Section across a Coral Reef, fringing the shore

It is in its external form that a coral reef shews features which give it an individuality above that of a mere heap of stones. Generally it rises with a steep slope from the sea bottom which ends in a low precipice, above which is another and more gentle slope to the highest point of the reef, a foot or two above lowest water, which is near its outer edge. Passing landwards the reef level is lower again, and we may have a boat channel or series of lagoons, where the native canoes can travel on calm water however the sea may rage outside. This is succeeded by a flat of bare rock, which rises slowly up to the base of the undercut coral cliffs as in imaginary section in Diagram 1 and the Photograph on Plate XXXII.

We have here three striking features, viz. precipitous reef edge, raised border and reef flat with boat channel, strongly

Plate XXXII

Fig. 71. Undercut cliffs of Rawaya. The whole foreground is reef flat
formed by the planing down of the land

differentiating the shore of a coral sea from the more or less even slope we are accustomed to at home, resulting in a nearly waveless shore and breakers out at sea, an endless line of purest white dividing the green of the shallows from the blue-black of the deep water.

Imagine land newly raised from the sea upon which coral growth is only beginning. In section its coastline would be a more or less gradual slope (to take the simplest case) as the line A, B in Diagram 2, sea level being represented by the line C, D. Suppose the scale to be such that the depth C to A is about 50 fathoms. Now it is found that under the best of conditions reef corals do not grow at this depth; if the conditions are less favourable so the maximum depth at which

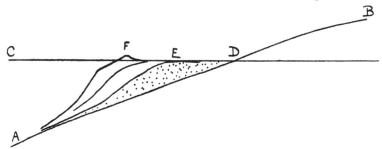

Diagram 2. The Commencement of a Reef

these corals grow is decreased. (That this fact is the crux of the problems to be discussed later may as well be noted at once.) Coral growth will be most luxuriant in the shallow water, and the first stage of our reef will be a mound of coral of the shape shewn in section by the dotted area. Between E and D this comes to the surface, and the corals, projecting above the water at lowest spring tides, are killed at the top, so that E to D becomes an almost flat surface of dead corals, some of which may, however, be still living where their bases are immersed in clear sea-water. A continuation of this process gives us a reef flat of considerable area, indicated by the line F, D, the slope A, F becoming correspondingly steepened. At the point F the waves have thrown up a long low mound of coral fragments and shells, which, in the way described below, may be consolidated into a ridge of solid rock.

It is easy to see how an extension of coral growth would make A, F a regular precipice, as F approximates to C. What happens after F, the reef edge, grows out to water 50 fathoms deep, where no living foundation can be laid for

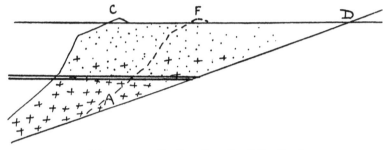

Diagram 3. Further Growth of the Reef

the support of the still growing reef above? Diagram 3 explains. Passing seawards from F is the gentle slope formed by the breaking waves, next a precipice, followed by a very steep slope to the sea bottom beyond A formed of the broken and dead corals fallen from the growing zone above, and which forms the foundation on which the shallow water corals extend the reef seawards.

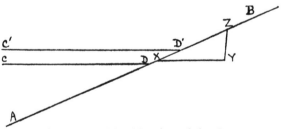

Diagram 4. The Abrasion of the Coast

Now at the same time as growth has added to the reef seawards the waves have cut down the land on the other side. Consider this case separately and then combine with that above. As before, A, B in Diagram 4 is the outline in section of recently formed land upon which the sea has as yet had no action, and C, D is the level of lowest tides, C′, D′ that of the highest. Between these two levels, upon the land mass lying between D and D', is the never ceasing beat of waves and the wear of silt-carrying currents, so that in time the land is eaten away along a line a little above C, D, say X, Y, and a cliff, Y, Z, is formed. We are assuming that the material of the land is sufficiently coherent to form such a flat and cliff, but even so in general X, Y becomes a sloping shore, not a flat. It only remains as a flat if for some reason the seaward surface at X is protected against further detrition by waves, e.g. by the growth of corals and stony seaweeds. If they are present, even if their growth adds nothing to the mass of the rock, it hinders its decay and causes the formation of a reef flat in place of a sloping shore.

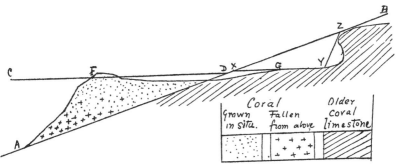

Diagram 5. Formation of fringing reef partly by growth of coral, partly by cutting down of land

Now these two processes, addition by growth and abrasion by wave action, go on simultaneously, and to get at the true method of formation of a reef flat in the Red Sea the two diagrams must be combined, as in Diagram 5, where as before F is the raised reef edge and F, Y the whole extent of the reef flat, and the cliff Z, Y is undermined as shewn. Where, as in some seas, F to D is recent growth and X to Y is rather older coral rock, it is impossible to locate accurately the dividing line between reef formed by recent growth and that cut out of the land, but near shore, where the flat is free from mud and sand, its surface is seen to consist of *sections* of the constituent shells and corals, cut as cleanly as if done by a stonemason (see Plate XXXIII). Even such hard shells as those of the "giant clam," *Tridacna*, are cut across at the same level, thus shewing very clearly the origin of the surface by the planing down of a mass of rock to that level.

The boat channel indicated between F and G remains to be accounted for. As the reef flat widens it results in a great area covered by shallow water at high tide level and partly bare at low. Exposed to a tropic sun life is impossible for any but a few specialised forms, the rock is unprotected from such wave motion as there is, and from boring organisms, which agencies quickly reduce its level. Strong currents also flow over the surface, for the breakers throw water over the raised edge which may have to travel several miles before reaching a gap through which it can return to the sea, and this with tidal currents cause swift rivers of muddy water to flow over the reef flat parallel with the shore. The obvious result is the hollowing out of a boat channel[1], and the accumulation in it of great quantities of mud and sand, which in many places form the greater part of its actual surface, but which eventually are swept out to sea.

The presence of certain marine flowering plants of grass-like form (*Cymodocea* and other genera) assists, if not wholly responsible for, the formation of such accumulations by binding the mass together by their strong and tangled roots and rhizomes.

When the channel has become broad and deep enough, coral growth may resume sway in it, sometimes to such an extent as almost to block it up again.

I need offer no proof of the formation of a reef flat and precipice by coral growth, the thing is obvious, at least in the

---

[1] Owing to the practical absence of tide in the Red Sea the boat channels of the fringing reef are discontinuous, so that at intervals the canoe men must wait for favourable weather and put out to the open sea. In Zanzibar, e.g., one can travel the whole 60 miles of the east coast within the reef but for the crossing of one bay, except at lowest spring tides. Some of the deeper parts of the boat channel of Red Sea reefs are due to faulting (see next chapter) as may be also a very peculiar reef channel just north of Mombasa Harbour.

Plate XXXIII

Fig. 72. A portion of a reef flat shewing *sections* of contained shells

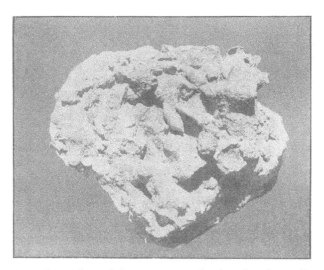

Fig. 73. The under surface of the same stone shewing that the reef is composed of a loosely cohering mass of shells and broken coral. In the centre of the mass is a shell easily recognisable as one living in abundance nowadays, *Strombus fasciatus*

case of ordinary fringing reefs. But the hollowing out of the boat channel, and with it that of other lagoons enclosed by coral, is less obvious, and it is natural to assign to a feature so distinctive of coral reefs an origin more directly dependent on the laws of coral growth. The proof comes from a consideration of the simplest case. Do we know of any reefs where solution and abrasion have formed these characteristic features without aid from coral growth? We do.

The east coast of the island of Zanzibar is, like that of the Sudan on the Red Sea, composed entirely of elevated coral. But for some reason this abundant growth ceased shortly after the elevation of the island, and the reef edge bears now nothing but a little stony and filamentous seaweed, and in deeper water forests of sea-grass (*Cymodocea*). The reef is very wide, up to three miles, the edge regularly raised, and boat channel, as above mentioned, generally well developed. On the raised edge of the reef are numbers of stones, a foot or two in diameter, composed of the same recrystallised coral rock[1] as the shores and cliffs of the island. Now this rock differs very widely from that formed of recent coral in its hardness and weight. Its specific gravity totally forbids the assumption that these stones were torn from the reef by breakers and cast up in their present position above low tide level and indeed, though constantly among them and turning them over to search for specimens of marine life, I never saw one that had recently been moved by the waves, much less broken away from some projection of the submarine precipice.

In fact these are the hardest remnants of the mass of rock which has been removed in the cutting out of the reef, and their presence proves (1) that this was the mode of formation of the reefs, (2) that the addition by growth taking place since the elevation of the old reef has been either nothing or very inconsiderable. Here solution, attrition, and boring organisms alone have carved out from dead

[1] For the qualities and formation of this rock see page 111.

rock all the features of a reef which has grown up un-
disturbed[1].

The present flora of the reef edge may have been preceded by a flora and fauna capable of affording a more
efficient protection, as is at present the case in the adjacent
and similar island of Pemba, where the reef is narrower and
consequently cleaner, and some stunted corals and *Tubipora*
grow on the outer slope of the reef edge, a position where
such species are never found in Zanzibar.

The absence of corals from the outer slope of the reef
edge is remarkable seeing that they flourish in a few places in
the boat channel, so much so in one place as to almost block
it up and form a new reef surface. They flourish too round
all the many sandbanks and islets of the channel which
separates Zanzibar from the mainland of Africa. The mud
from the broad reef flat together with the strong currents that
impinge upon these coasts are amply sufficient to prevent the
settlement of the delicate coral larvae, if not to destroy full-
grown colonies.

Another case from the Cape Verde Islands, where reef
corals do not exist at all, is shewn on Plate XXXIV. A reef
flat, with raised definite edge and miniature boat channel
complete, has been cut out of sandstone, the edge of which
was protected by a growth of stony seaweed (lithothamnia),
and vast numbers of the shelly tubes of that strange animal
Vermetus[2]. These two organisms combine to form a continuous crust over the whole surface of the seaward edge of

---

[1] The absence of similar stones from all other parts of the reef is to be
accounted for by their being subject to the continual friction of strong sand-laden
currents, while those on the raised edge are exposed to waves of clean water for
a portion of each day only.

[2] These tubes form a mass by coiling loosely together like a cluster of worms,
though the animal which makes them is exactly like those that have regular spiral
shells and move about freely, e.g. the whelks. The young *Vermetus* has a shell
like a young whelk, but as it then fixes itself down, the shell degenerates, and
grows into the loosely coiled tube of the adult mollusc. Nothing could be more
different than the body of a *Vermetus* and that of a worm, the resemblances
between the shell of the one and the tube of the other being pure coincidence.

Plate XXXIV

Fig. 74. A sandstone reef near St Vincent, Cape Verde Islands

Fig. 75. An embryo fringing reef near Ramleh, Alexandria

the sandstone, and so greatly delay its removal by the sea, but landwards, this protection being absent, the reef flat is hollowed out into a "boat channel." This sandstone is a local deposit just to the south-west of the town of St Vincent, but the volcanic rocks of which the island is composed are cut down to a narrow flat in the same way, but less regularly.

A third case, from the Mediterranean near Alexandria, is so striking as to be worth illustrating, though only the embryo of a reef, as it were a ledge a few yards wide, has been formed as yet. The rock is a calcareous sandstone, a consolidated dune, and the protecting organisms are much the same as those found in the Cape Verde Islands, but here forming a less coherent coating to the rock. The regularity of the ledge laid bare by the retreat of a wave is very striking.

Reefs may shew other features, no one arrangement can be taken as typical of all. Instead of the smooth slope and rounded ridge which compose the reef edge on this coast and that of Zanzibar it is usual, in many oceanic reefs, for the growing edge to be cut into by deep and narrow fissures, up which the great breakers send violent torrents of water.

The land, or reef islands, may be either portions of the reef elevated above sea level, containing fossil corals in the positions in which they grow, or it may be partly formed of a mass of corals thrown up by storms backed generally by an accumulation of sand. The coral rock thus elevated may be, as in the Red Sea, but little different from the original material of which it was formed, but more generally it is much altered. The continual wetting by spray or rain and drying under the tropical sun has a very marked effect in hardening and consolidating elevated coral, or coral sand. The upper parts are dissolved, and as the water sinks into the porous corals and becomes supersaturated with lime, the latter is crystallised out, thus filling up all cavities with *crystalline* limestone. Thus in the end the highly porous heterogeneous limestone becomes a rock of exceeding hardness, crystalline and homogeneous. All the more delicate organisms are dissolved, only the largest remaining recognisable. At the same time as sea-water contains magnesium carbonate as well as limestone, and the former is less soluble than the latter, it tends to be deposited more quickly, so that it comes to replace the original limestone to some extent[1]. The alteration in the external appearance of the rock is very marked. Instead of the yellow, rather shapeless, cliffs of the Red Sea coast, in most other parts of the world, where tides supply spray and there is a considerable rainfall, we have coal-black rock with a very peculiar surface, all covered with sharp points and knife edges separating depressions left by the solution of the stone by water, hence the name "coral rag" applied to such rock. Where it forms the shore of a sheltered bay its homogeneity causes the undermining by the sea to go on to an astonishing extent before the unsupported piece falls away from the cliff to which it is attached. Such projections of the rocks which may be much longer than those shewn on Plate XXXV, also illustrate the hardness of this recrystallised material, for on striking one with a hammer a loud clear bell-like note is produced. Given the right conditions and we have the same peculiar result in the Red Sea and even in the Mediterranean. For instance, a considerable swell breaks at times on the narrow reef fringing the east side of the Tella Tella Kebir Islands, thus keeping the cliff behind it drenched with spray. In consequence the rock has become like that of Zanzibar and British East Africa. And generally, wherever the coral rock is exposed to spray it takes on these characters partially or completely, as is the case at the bases of all the cliffs along a narrow band just about sea level, where the rock is "'twixt wind and water." Here the outer part is converted into a black, hard, and pitted crust, higher up it is harder than normal but above gradually passes into the slightly altered rock of the normal cliffs. Such a

[1] More correctly a *compound*, not mixture of carbonates, is formed, viz. dolomite, $CaMg(CO_3)_2$.

Plate XXXV

Figs. 76 and 77.   Coral Cliffs, Zanzibar

Fig. 76.   Chuaka Bay.   Note undermining of fallen fragments

„   77.   Bawi Island.   Rock masses supported by narrow stalks

crust also covers the reef flats of the Red Sea, the reef within consisting, as before noted, of loose masses of coral bedded in with shells and sand. A portion of this crust is photographed on Plate XXXIII; the upper surface (Fig. 72) with its *sections* of contained shells has already been referred to. It is nearly smooth and very hard. The under side of the same fragment is shewn in the next figure and is seen to consist of an irregular mass of shells and coral branches lightly cemented to the crust, from between which the sand, which has not been consolidated, has fallen away. The formation of beach sandstone is practically the same process of cementation, by alternate solution and deposition of lime, taking place in a mass of shell and coral sand instead of larger fragments, the rock following exactly the curve of the sandbank, of which it is obviously a part which has been consolidated *in situ.*

Coral reefs are classified into three sets according to their relation with other land[1].

I. *Fringing reefs*, which, as the name implies, border the land, are continuous with it, and the seaward edge of which can be reached by wading.

II. *Barrier reefs*, which run parallel to the coast but separated from it by deep water navigable for coasting vessels larger than canoes.

III. *Atolls*, ring- or crescent-shaped reefs having no obvious relation to any land and typically found far out in the ocean, from the great depths of which they rise with steep slopes to, at most, a few feet above high tide level.

Fringing reefs we have already dealt with; the two agents described—growth and abrasion of coral—will account for all of them. Barriers and atolls are more puzzling. Why should the barrier form its line parallel to the coast, though at a distance from it, and the very existence of atolls is one of the most striking phenomena of Nature.

The problem is complicated by the fact that ordinary reef corals die out at a depth of 50 fathoms or so. Now 50

---

[1] Examples of all three are well shewn on the map opposite page 136.

fathoms is a mere nothing compared to the depths from which the Pacific atolls rise, and is only a quarter the depth often found within a few hundred yards of the Red Sea reefs. How then to account for the building of reefs in deep water?

One suggestion was that atoll rings were formed by the growth of a mere cap of coral round the edge of the craters of huge submarine volcanoes. But that postulates far too large a number of such immense volcanoes[1], and the early stages of these formations have not been found. Darwin's hypothesis was hailed with joy as the obvious solution, and held the field against all rivals for many years. Briefly it is that corals formed a reef by direct growth in shallow water on the coast of an island, forming a fringe thereto in the way explained above. Now is postulated one of those great, slow earth movements such as have very often occurred in the past and are occurring at the present day. In this case the island is to sink slowly, at such a rate that the reef grows upwards as fast as it is submerged. The result is obviously a mass of corals of a thickness equal to the total sinking movement of our island, though every individual coral grew while in water under 50 fathoms deep.

When our island is half submerged the fringing reef has become a barrier, when wholly gone the reef ring remains enclosing an empty lagoon, and is the only mark of the grave of a drowned island. Thus Darwin's theory has the further merit of referring the two forms of reef, barrier and atoll, to one common cause, the sinking of the land. But we have no idea of how the original islands were formed in such numbers, and many believe that no such vast sinking of the ocean basins has occurred since they were formed. Also, if solution be ignored, it is difficult to see why, as the island sank, coral growth did not close in over the submerged land, and so form a vast reef flat instead of leaving a lagoon up to 50 fathoms deep.

To settle the matter an expedition was sent to a typical atoll, Funafuti, and a boring 1200 feet deep was made to find

---

[1] I.e. in the great oceans. As shewn later, volcanic mounds and islands are found in the Red Sea, and may have formed the foundations of certain of its reefs.

out what the interior of the reef is made of. The material brought out of the bore hole has been carefully examined by experts, and reported to consist of the remains of exactly similar corals to those found near the surface, and this result was taken by one or two geologists as complete vindication of Darwin's theory. But apart from the extreme difficulty of the identification of all coral species, especially those which have been subject to partial crystallisation and so on, one remembers that a considerable part of the foundations in deep water are formed of corals which have fallen down the steep slope from the growing reef above, so that their presence buried a thousand fathoms deep proves nothing, while the boring at Funafuti only went to about 200 fathoms.

After all it is easier to imagine that the atoll grew up from the bottom of the deep sea. The only postulate is a chance elevation on the sea bottom. On such elevations it is found that the remains of marine organisms, including deep sea corals (as distinct from reef builders), tend to accumulate much more rapidly than on the floor of the surrounding depths. The elevation is con-sequently slowly but surely raised, and the higher it grows the more rapid the accumulation, until at last reef corals obtain a footing forming a cap or pinnacle reaching to the surface. From this masses of coral, sand, stones or large boulders, are always falling on to the foundation slopes, forming successive sloping layers in-

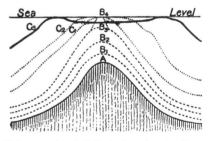

Diagram 6. Original elevation A of sea bottom shaded, B_1—B_4 additions formed by growth, C_1—C_3 slopes of coral &c. fallen from above. The thick line of C_3 is outline of section of the atoll mass resulting.

dicated by the dotted lines, upon which fresh growth takes its rise[1]. When the coral reef has become of some breadth

---

[1] Gardiner, J. S., "The building of Atolls," *Proc. Camb. Phil. Soc.* or The Challenger Society's *Science of the Sea*, John Murray.

(and atoll rings may be 30 miles or more across) a boring at the edge might descend for a thousand fathoms and never meet with the original foundations, but would pass only through recent corals fallen from the shallow zone.

We should expect to find a continuous surface of coral at sea level. As a matter of fact there is a broad lagoon, generally of considerable depth, one or two gaps through the encircling reef giving communication with the open ocean. This is the natural result of the causes described when dealing with the boat channel of a fringing reef; it is the same thing on a much larger scale. Seeing that the rate of growth of coral masses is always only the excess of growth over destruction and solution, the presence of growing corals is no evidence against the fact that the lagoon shores may be undergoing destruction, and that such coral growth as is present may add nothing to the inner sides of the reef in the end. No more does the accumulation of great quantities of mud prove that the lagoon will in time be quite filled in. Mud and sand[1] are but stages in the destruction of coral rock, and its presence where that process is going on is to be expected. An abnormal tide, a shift of the currents, and vast quantities are swept out through the gaps in the reefs. My home on the Red Sea is beside a large landlocked lagoon in which coral gardens of great luxuriance, whence collections of many species can be procured, are frequent. Spite of this, the evidence is as clear as possible that its shores and islands are undergoing rapid denudation, and its reefs are being cut down by currents to banks below water level. As in the Red Sea the level rarely alters by more than a foot once in the twenty-four hours, and often the rise or fall is much less, the action of tidal currents is at a minimum, yet even so they produce well-marked effects.

---

[1] In some lagoons quantities of sand are formed of great numbers of the minute shells of lowly organisms, the foraminifera. This is, of course, a very different thing to that resulting from breaking up of coral and shells.

Barrier reefs may be formed from fringing reefs by the enlargement of the boat channel, while the reef is extending seawards.

The island of Zanzibar, 60 miles long by 20 wide, and 20 miles from the mainland of Africa, seems to be a part of the East African barrier system, and it certainly was separated from the mainland by the destruction of the intervening land ; the shallow dividing channel being full of shoals and sandbanks formed by cutting down of islands. The fauna of Zanzibar, including leopards, serval cats, &c., can be accounted for in no other way. The Great Barrier of Australia, a thousand miles long, is the same thing on a vastly greater scale. But, as described in the next chapter, the Barrier system of the Red Sea is quite another thing, and its mode of formation may possibly be unique in the world.

CHAPTER IX

The Climate has already been roughly described but it is interesting enough to deal with in more detail.

One might suppose the extremes of dry heat and cold of the desert climate to be moderated by the sea, and the resulting mean to be a fairly mild and equable climate. Actually we get alternations of desert and sea climates, extreme dry heat in summer and steaming winds from the sea, both bringing great discomfort.

The winter from November to March is cool and pleasant so long as the prevailing north-east wind blows, but there are spells of very disagreeable weather even in winter. When the wind is from the south-east the temperature rises and at the same time it becomes very damp, saltish moisture being over everything, so that even the natives become lazy and depressed and many suffer from rheumatism, &c.

One has however the satisfaction of knowing that the south-east wind usually lasts but three days or so, and never more than a week, when the north wind comes back and we revive.

The south wind is generally preceded by a day's calm and increases in strength until the end, when a short calm ushers in a very strong wind from the north. On several occasions I have actually seen the approach of this sudden and welcome change as a line of low cloud, formed by the condensation of vapour where the cold north wind meets the damp from the south.

This sudden change was the cause of the wrecking of a *sambûk* which was beating down to Port Sudan in a south-east wind. Anchoring one night in a long narrow harbour open to the north,.they were caught by the north wind next morning and, being unable to beat out against it, were driven on to the reef. The crew had to walk in to Port Sudan, distant about twenty-five miles, without food or water, one of them having a badly crushed wrist. As I had cargo on the *sambûk* I went up immediately, and after only two or three days there was nothing visible of the *sambûk*, but fragments scattered over miles of reef.

In winter the desert wind, due north or a little west of north, is very much colder than the usual north-north-east. The mornings indeed may be quite chilly, and though this is very welcome to the Englishman the natives suffer considerably. On the first day or two of such a period the wind is strong, charged perhaps with sand, and so dry that the backs of books curl as if they had been before a fire.

In the summer the alternations of climate may be astonishingly rapid, both may occur on one hot-weather day in July or August as follows. The land breeze is very weak, and dies away about 6 a.m., when already the sun is blazing hot. By 8 a.m. it is intolerable, but as it is still dead calm pearlers and fishermen are at sea making use of their opportunity. If however they expect a day of "hurûr" or hot wind they do not go far away, and when warned by two or three preliminary puffs of wind off shore, they must make all haste to return, or risk being swept out to sea. In half an hour the wind may be furiously strong, heated as by a furnace and bearing dense clouds of fine dust, of the colour and density of a London fog, together with coarser sand that stings the face. Woe to one who has to travel against such a storm! The dry heat soon produces intolerable thirst, the eyes, nose and mouth are filled with sand, while one's face, eyelashes and even teeth are caked with mud produced by it with the natural moisture.

These conditions continue until noon, when a change may be expected, but may be deferred until 4 p.m., or rarely even 6 p.m. The wind suddenly ceases, the world becomes again visible, and the temperature drops from say 105° F. to 95° F. But soon there comes the reverse wind, almost equally strong, from the sea, and the humidity increases so much that the fall of temperature is not the relief that might be expected, being but the change from oven to steam-kettle. The natives tell me that this wind, so hot in the plains, among the mountains is cold, and is heated by its passage over the sun-roasted plains. Apparently the great heat here originates miniature local cyclones, cold air from the mountain tops, or drawn *over* the mountains, rushing down to fill the low pressure area on the plains, being heated there and rushing on a few miles out to sea, whence the easterly return wind originates. At Dongonab these "hurûr" winds are rarer than they are further south, where they are of almost daily occurrence during the summer, while at Halaib, 100 miles further north, the natives tell me they do not occur at all. Consequently we are sometimes visited by the return wind in the morning, caused by "hurûr" at a point further down the coast. Such a cyclone is illustrated by the frontispiece, which represents the combination of thunder clouds over the mountains while a "hurûr" rages over the plain and for several miles out to sea. But among the barrier reefs, though the wind is blowing directly towards them, all is glassy calm.

The rainfall is extremely scanty and local, though markedly better in the south, where the population is correspondingly greater and the fauna richer.

There are two seasons when rain may be hoped for, viz. the "kharîf" which centres round August, and which is referred to in the frontispiece, and the winter months, but if rain fell for an hour or two on three days it would be considered a liberal supply for the whole year in most places. At Dongonab there has been no rain (above a millimetre or two) since December, 1907, though one or two showers have fallen on Rawaya and Makawar[1]. There is of course much more rain on the hills than on the plains, but even so grass grows only in scattered areas to which the people migrate.

Tides. The Red Sea undergoes considerable variations of level at its extremities, up to seven feet at Suez, but in the middle the variations are small, only a few centimetres at Port Sudan. At Dongonab the difference between .highest and lowest levels recorded is 80 cm., but the maximum change in any 24 hours is rarely over 30 cm. Records shew a distinct tide, but this may be interfered with by changes of level due to wind and changes of atmospheric pressure, and in any case one of the usual two tides of the 24 hours is practically suppressed, the water remaining near high tide level until it falls for next day's tide. In the summer the average level is lower than in winter and the tidal effects are partially masked by the results of the peculiar climatic conditions. The water may remain low for days, so that all the coral which has grown above that level since the last occasion of extreme low water, which may have been one or even two years ago, dies off.

I suppose that every school-boy looking at an atlas, is struck by the peculiar shape of the Red Sea, and is led to ponder on the usefulness of this peculiar canal, the sole value of which is that it gives communication between Europe and the East, a value which needed but the trifling addition possible to human effort to make it the great highway of the world. Its own shores are desolate wastes, in itself it has no attraction for traffic, and even its shape seems to indicate that it is but a passage to other seas. (See map inside the cover.)

For so narrow a sea, only a little over a hundred miles wide, the depth is great, two hundred to five hundred fathoms at the side and a thousand in the middle. These peculiarities are also well marked in the deep Gulf of Akaba which bounds Sinai on the east—the Gulf of Suez, on the west, being a

---

[1] 1912 was a rich year! 40 millimetres fell on Oct. 22nd and 20 millimetres in December, about 2½ inches altogether.

shallower branch valley. Both these gulfs, like the Red Sea, are bounded on either side by high mountains, and those of the southern part of Sinai are particularly grand in the savage barrenness of their jagged peaks and vast precipices.

The Gulf of Akaba is directly in line with the Jordan Valley, a similar depression on a smaller scale, only partially occupied by water, the Dead Sea, while southwards we find another dry valley running through British East Africa and adjoining territories, a great trough bounded by plateaux, several thousand feet above its bottom. We can thus trace

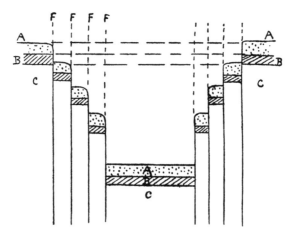

Diagram 7. Formation of a rift valley

this trough-like valley from Palestine to some degrees south of the Equator as a stupendous crack in the earth's surface, well named "The Great Rift Valley[1]." The Red Sea is its greatest section, its total depth here being, say, 5000 feet from the summit of the mountains[2] to sea level and 6000 feet to the sea bottom, 11,000 feet in all.

The formation of such a valley, by the dropping down of a series of strips of country below the level of the remainder, is illustrated by Diagram 7. To study the simplest possible

---

[1] J. W. Gregory, *The Great Rift Valley*, John Murray, 1896.
[2] The ranges bordering the sea are from 4000 feet to 8000 feet high, but of course were much higher in the days when the Rift opened.

case we draw a section through the ground and imagine it formed of three kinds of rock, of which two form horizontal sheets, AA and BB, over the third CC. These were originally unbroken, and in the positions shewn by the lines of dashes, but were broken by the dropping down of the central part to form the valley shewn here in section. The floor of the valley has the same structure as the original surface of the ground, the same three beds, A, B and C, occurring in the same positions, but at a lower level. They are found again in each of the steps on the valley's sides, their regular reappearance in this way being conclusive proof of the earth movements postulated.

The vertical lines FFFF, between each step and the next drop, along which the continuity of the beds is broken, are termed "faults," a geological term which should be remembered.

Rift valleys are found elsewhere in the world, but are exceptional, ordinary valleys, with their winding courses and rounded outlines, having been formed by the action of streams, which slowly wash away the ground and hollow out their courses to the sea.

The actual structure of the middle portion of the Red Sea Valley is shewn diagrammatically by the section on page 145. Five steps are shewn, Nos. 2 and 3 being further separated by a minor fault valley. The details are described later.

The southern part of the sea, below Masawa, has recently been subjected to volcanic[1] action ; many of the islands there are quite well-preserved volcanic cones, but as regards the rest of the sea, though earth movements have been frequent and considerable, there are now no traces of volcanic action, and the movements that have occurred have not necessarily involved cataclysms greater than severe earthquakes.

There are however in the north two islands the existence of which is most readily explained by volcanic action. I refer to the coral formations known as "The Brothers" and

---

[1] Recently, that is, geologically speaking.

"Daedalus Shoal," the former a pair of low islets, the latter a flat reef, rising out of the centre of the sea and surrounded by water hundreds of fathoms deep. They are extremely steep-sided cones, and what could form and support such structures far out from land is puzzling. A certain view of another section of the Rift Valley, that once seen can never be forgotten, seems to offer an explanation. After passing through the forests of the Kikuyu Plateau by the Uganda Railway one comes out into the open on the brink of the great escarpment of the Rift Valley and looks across a trough 3000 feet deep to the similar forest-clad heights of the Mau on the other side. The continuity of the valley is rudely broken by two volcanic cones rising abruptly in the middle of the flat bottom of the trough. On consideration the strangeness of their appearance in the middle of a valley passes away, one sees that the bottom of such a rift must be a zone of weakness of the earth's crust where volcanoes might naturally be expected to arise.

If the water were removed from the Red Sea Valley would not the appearance of The Brothers and Daedalus be very much like that of the two volcanoes of British East Africa, allowing for the steeper angle at which their materials would lie under water? Given such cones of loose volcanic ash, &c., wave action would quickly level down their summits until coral growth afforded

Diagram 8. Formation of atoll as a cap of coral growing on a mound of loose volcanic material. A original mound, B as cut down by the sea, C the atoll.

protection and formed a cap of rock, part of which is now raised again above sea level as the islands on one of which the lighthouse is built.

The ring-shaped reef of Sanganeb[1], opposite Port Sudan, which is outside the Barrier system and separated from it by

---

[1] Such ring-shaped reefs, rising out of deep water, are termed Atolls. Sanganeb is a small example compared to those of the Indian and Pacific Oceans.

water 400 fathoms deep, may be built on a similar foundation. Like the two coral reefs above it rises with extremely steep slopes from this deep water, and is the summit of a submarine pinnacle rather than hill.

On the other hand, the foundations of these strangely isolated reefs may be like a certain island which, rising high above sea level, shews its structure, a centre of olivine rock fringed with coral. This island is variously known as Zeberjed, St Johns, and Emerald Island, the latter name due to its possession of mines for peridots, which are worked by the Khedive of Egypt. Its position is 23° 30' N., distant about 60 miles from the African coast, a formation quite independent of the sides of the Rift Valley. It is an example of the "Block Mountains" described by Professor Gregory, portions of the original earth surface which have remained standing when the surrounding country dropped down to form the trough of the Rift Valley, not a mass of land thrust upwards and subsequently carved into peaks and valleys by running water, which is the way ordinary mountain ranges are formed.

One gets a good idea of the structure of the Red Sea coasts on leaving the Gulf of Suez for the voyage south, before the ship's course passes far from land. On the western horizon is a range of wild mountains, a grey plain ending in a yellow shore-line separating them from the sea, and the off-lying islands are of the same colour. The plain is formed of gravel from the high hills, its yellow border seawards being coral limestone, and the islands also. In the sea are numerous reefs, here of very intricate plan, lines of white breakers separating the deep blue black water from large areas of green and brown shoals in waveless lagoons. There are deep channels between these reefs and the shore, which is itself fringed by a shallow reef with its edge at low water level but bearing perhaps one or two fathoms of water on its surface within.

This being the simple structure of both sides of the whole

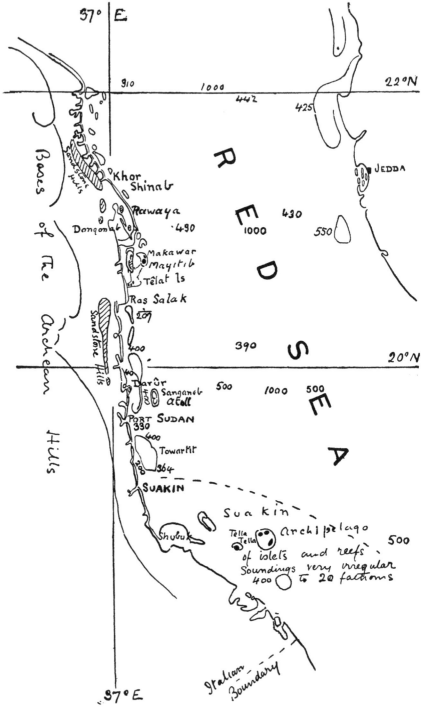

Fig. 78. Coast of the Anglo-Egyptian Sudan

Sandstone hills shaded, *small* islands black. Coastline double, the outer line being the edge of the fringing reef. The thin lines enclosing roughly oval or elongated areas at sea are the barrier reefs. Figures on sea represent depths in fathoms.

Red Sea trough I may proceed to describe in detail one section of the coast, that bounding the territory of the Anglo-Egyptian Sudan, between 18° and 22° N. This section includes two (Ras Rawaya and Ras Salak) of the three promontories which break the straight line of the west coast north of Masawa, the third being Ras Benas, further north. The map opposite shews clearly the fringing reef which lies along the whole coastline, the numerous harbours, of which Port Sudan, Suakin, and Trinkitat are of commercial importance[1], the deep channel separating the fringing from the barrier reefs, and the atoll of Sanganeb on which the lighthouse is built.

On land the bases of the high mountains are indicated, and certain lower hills, of sandstone, which rise in the midst of the maritime plain. A striking fact is visible on first inspection of this map, viz. that not only is the Red Sea a nearly parallel-sided trough but that the constituents of the sides are themselves placed in lines parallel to the coast. The Archean hills[2], the lesser sandstone ranges, the coral bounding the maritime plain, and the barrier reefs, are all four roughly parallel to the main axis of the sea.

We will consider each feature in more detail. For the Archean hills consult the extremely interesting memoirs of the Egyptian Geological Survey[3]; for our purposes it is enough to note that they are all of ancient igneous and metamorphic rocks, that they rise to heights of from four to eight thousand feet, and the valley bottoms are generally flat and filled in with gravel.

The maritime plain is from five to ten miles wide, sloping up regularly from the sea towards the bases of the hills,

---

[1] I have marked other harbours as they are interesting geologically, but there are only three miserable villages on this whole coast in addition to the two towns. There is no village at Trinkitat, but the cotton from Tokar is loaded on to *sambûks* here.

[2] I.e. hills of Archean, ancient rock, as opposed to the newer sandstones, gravels and limestones.

[3] The Eastern Desert of Egypt, southern section, describes a part of the Red Sea coast range north of the Sudan boundary, but essentially similar to the rest.

where it may attain a level of several hundred feet. Except at its seaward edge, it is composed of black gravel, the product of the decay of the hills carried down by the torrents resulting from the rare but furious rain-storms, and spread out to form the plain. Sand-hills occur, but not very commonly, though the gravel is mingled with sand throughout, and in sections of the plain exposed by wells, layers of gravel alternate with sand, fine or coarse, as far as the deepest borings have been carried[1].

The pebbles, though black predominate, are of a most remarkable variety of kinds and colours. Bright green and red, yellow and clear white are abundant, and any square yard would yield a rich collection in Petrology. As the torrents open out into the level plain they lose themselves, continually taking to fresh channels, so that the *débris* from series of hills quite distant from one another are mingled; in a given spot gravel from one valley is laid down this year, from another and totally distinct one another. One would expect gravel which had been carried by torrents a distance of many miles to be rounded down by friction into smooth boulders or pebbles, like those of our home streams. As a matter of fact it is nearly always angular, the rounded surfaces we should expect being rarely met with on the surface. The pebbles, as we now see them, have been re-formed from larger stones since their transport through the valleys and over the plain. Large stones, lying half buried in smaller material, shew the usual rounded surfaces of water-borne rock, but they are invariably split up by fissures, which may be half an inch broad, so that the stone is as it were built up of angular fragments fitted together after the style of a puzzle picture. During the hundreds of years they have lain there, apparently secure from all interference, they have been exposed to innumerable fierce heats and cold nights, which, causing

---

[1] Two borings, made in the hope of obtaining water two miles inland, near Port Sudan, were carried down through 300 metres, nearly 1000 feet, of this kind of material.

Plate XXXVI

Fig. 79. The maritime plain and Irba Mountains

Yemêna oasis in foreground and gravel-covered ridge across middle distance

Plate XXXVII

Figs. 80 and 81. Corals, in position of growth, on the summit
of Jebel Têtâwib

successive minute expansions and contractions, have at last split the stones into small pieces. This is the origin of the irregularly shaped gravel; first indeed it was rounded by the grinding and pounding of the torrents of hundreds of successive winters, then it was split up again by the silent invisible stresses of heat and cold.

The accumulation of this vast mass of gravel and sand in the manner described has taken a length of time compared to which a human life is but a moment. Even from the geological point of view it has been not inconsiderable. There is abundant evidence that the plain was formed, much as it is now, at a time when the coast-line was entirely different, and though there is no good evidence of the country's having been other than desert throughout historical time, there probably was a greater rainfall when the formation of the plain was in full swing.

The sandstone hills are particularly interesting in that one finds a regular layer of coral on their summits, which shews that they were once nearly level with the sea, and are in fact coral reefs which have been elevated to heights of from 100 to 1000 feet. In some of those hills to which I have had access the corals on the summit are wonderfully well preserved, and by this fact, and that the species are indistinguishable from those now living in the sea, prove the elevation of the hills to have been geologically recent. Further, the larger coral colonies are at once seen to be still in the position in which they grew, not tilted or overthrown in any way. This is not the case with the older rocks on which they lie, the strata of which are frequently twisted and broken, and this is particularly noticeable sometimes in the case of the layer of gypsum which is often found between the coral and the sandstone (Fig. 89 on page 144).

The hills are not marked on any map, indeed no survey has yet been made hereabouts. My account is therefore incomplete, but this does not invalidate the conclusions drawn. From seaward these hills are very easily distinguished from

c.

the jagged hills of archean rock, the true boundary of the Rift Valley, by their flat tops and the light yellow colour of their cliffs, and also by their generally being nearer the sea even than the great mounds of gravel which sometimes form the foot-hills of the mountain range.

Passing from south to north the first range is met with a few miles north of Mersa[1] Durûr, as a chain of low butts rising from the alluvial plain a few miles inland. These become higher and more continuous as one passes northwards, culminating in two considerable hills, of about the same height and area of base, the northern of which is marked on the charts, where it is called Table Mountain, and given a height of 1000 feet.

At about five miles inland from Dongonab are a couple of small hills standing alone, but a little farther north lying inland from the middle of the North Basin of Dongonab Bay is a considerable range, extending towards the hills about Khor Shinab, Hamama, &c., from which it is separated by an interval of only a few miles.

The Abu Hamâma[2] range (which I so name from its most prominent though not highest peak, a landmark for sailors) extends from about the inner branches of Khor Shinab to some distance beyond Khor Abu Hamâma, lying much nearer the sea than do the others. Its height is estimated by a government surveyor at from 500 to 700 feet. (Map, p. 126.)

These ranges are wholly inland, and rise from the maritime plain, which they divide longitudinally. The scattered ranges of sandstone are not the whole of this formation however. I give a view of a part of the maritime plain in which it is seen to rise as a distinct fold across the middle distance. This appears to consist of the usual gravel, but where cut into by the Yemêna ravine a very different state of things is

---

[1] "Mersa" in Arabic=anchorage.

[2] Arabic Hamâma=pigeon. The shape of this hill is a cone with a cubical block on its apex, hence the appropriate name Pigeon Hill. "Khor" is used for an inlet of the sea, among other meanings.

Plate XXXVIII

Fig. 82. Water-hole under a stratum of hard gravel and gypsum
conglomerate, in the lower part of the ravine

Fig. 83. Exposure of *sandstone* under the gravel of the plain
Two views in Yemêna ravine, which cuts the maritime plain

displayed. It is practically all sandstone, covered by a few feet of gravel and gypsum conglomerate. Of coral I only saw one large boulder, having no time for a search. There is yet another range rising from the sea, namely two small hills on the peninsula of Rawaya, and the islands of Makawar and Mayitib, of which Makawar is the only considerable elevation. This range is of special interest and will be described in detail.

Coral of the coast-line.

This band of elevated coral is never very wide, about a mile at Suakin, exclusive of the reef, and rather less at Port Sudan. At Suakin, and to the south it is very slightly raised above sea level, but at Port Sudan and generally to the north it is from 10—20 feet higher, and is separated from the gravel plain by a depression a few hundred yards wide. This depression is often very near sea level and floored with mud in which grow the plants of salt marshes.

Although to the ordinary non-scientific person the idea that most land was once beneath the sea, and nearly all rocks were formed beneath the water, may be known, yet unfamiliar, no one can land on these coral shores without being specially and personally impressed by the fact that, as the ground is entirely formed of corals and shells it has been raised up from the sea, beneath which it was formed. One may walk about on a limestone hill in England and, by patient collection of fossils, partially corroborate the geologist's assertion that the whole thing is a mass of ancient shells, squeezed together and finally thrust up from the sea bottom, but here, so fresh are the shells, so familiar their forms and so abundant the coral, often complete in all its delicate detail[1] (like those figured opposite pages 88 and 91) that every man may be his own

---

[1] Actually many of these shells retain some of their colour ! e.g. the red of the common *Spondylus*, the bands of *Strombus fasciatus* and the mottlings of *Cyprina tigrina* are quite distinct on some specimens from 100 feet above, and on others dug out 15 feet below sea level.

geologist and assert the origin of the rock as a matter of personal knowledge. Further, he may assert that all the shells and most of the corals[1] are exactly like those now living on the Red Sea reefs, and so deduce the fact that the uplifting of the original coral reef has been geologically recent, long ages since the successive worlds of species of animal whose remains make up the older, and to British minds, more usual, limestones had, one after another, passed away and been finally replaced by the inhabitants of our own world.

It is one of the most recent of rocks, and yet it gives some idea of the meaning of the expression "Geologic time" to remember that these very ordinary-looking shells lived thousands of years before the builders of the pyramids.

We can better appreciate the raw newness of the Red Sea cliffs if we digress a little to the comparison with the very different rocks of Equatorial East Africa and elsewhere which have however much the same origin. These latter are much more typical of elevated coral the world over, the Red Sea, owing to its nearly rainless climate, having peculiarly well preserved the corals of its raised reefs. Plate XXXV of cliffs in Zanzibar should be compared with the Red Sea rocks on Plates XXXII and XXXVII, and the comparison made in Chapter VIII, page 111, referred to. Of course the differences between the elevated coral of the Equatorial coast and that of the Red Sea might be due to the former being of greater age; though, if such a difference exists, as it is not considerable[2], we are led to lay more stress on the different physical conditions under which they are placed. These are that the equatorial rocks are exposed to a considerable rainfall, and, owing to the tides, to far more drenching by spray than are those of the Red Sea, resulting in the solution of the surface layers of

---

[1] *All* the corals are of existing species, but the identification is less easy than in the case of the shells.

[2] Such fossils as are found in the Equatorial rocks are recent species, and the fault harbours of the coast have not had time to lose altogether the peculiar characters of such structures under the influence of the rivers which enter them and the strong tidal currents.

the rock and the crystallisation of the dissolved limestone in all the cavities of the interior, thus making the rock both crystalline and homogeneous within, as before described.

Where the Red Sea rock is exposed to alternate wetting and drying the beginnings of this change are evident. All the way along the coast from sea level up to a few feet above that portion of the cliff which is undermined by the waves, the rock is harder and more homogeneous, but this is merely a local alteration due to the action of spray. I had opportunities of examining the internal structure of these cliffs both when the foundations of the quay walls were being dredged out and when the slipway was excavated at Port Sudan. In both cases I found that within the homogeneity of the outer crust disappeared completely, giving place to exactly the structure of a recent growing reef, the larger colonies of coral forming great boulders bedded into a loose mass composed of smaller species and the broken fragments of those more delicately branched. At a depth of five metres I picked out shells retaining almost perfectly the colours and appearance of their living relatives of the same species. The general colour of the excavation was grey, the colour of the mud which is formed by the disintegration of coral and shells by boring worms, molluscs and sponges.

The finding of beds of coral on the tops of the sandstone hills at heights of 500 feet and more above sea level, and the fact that dead coral and shells form the ground along the coast-line, are explained, as we have seen, by a general uplifting of the whole country whereby coral reefs have become dry land and even hill tops. The breadth of the maritime plain is another evidence of the same fact, for no such plain can be formed on a sinking coast-line; in such places the successive deposits of sand and gravel from the hills are submerged and the following form layers on the top of the preceding and cannot be carried out beyond them to form a plain.

As an example of such a sinking coast-line compare Norway, where the hills rise directly from the sea and the valleys have sunk below the water forming the characteristic fjords.

Startling though the thought of such changes of the relative levels of sea and land may be, they are of common occurrence, and always have been, in fact they are the commonplace of geological history everywhere. Our present case is a movement of very minor degree, involving but a few hundred feet, a mere detail of the opening of that stupendous fissure, the Rift Valley, of which the whole Red Sea is but a portion.

It is interesting to note how very regular this elevation has been, entirely without twisting or contortion of the strata, so that the individual corals remain exactly in the same position, relative to the surrounding rock, as they did when growing on the reef.

Hence also the almost perfect level of the coast-line, which, spite of "faulting" by which a few small areas rise to a higher level as hills, and the opening of fissures, preserves the same level, within 20 feet, for several hundred miles. At the same time the elevation has been effected in several stages, as evidenced by the existence of level parallel lines of cliff along the sides of hills, e.g. Jebel Zêt in the Gulf of Suez, Jebel Makawar on the Sudan coast, which were cut out by the sea when the hills were at lower levels, and by successive beds of coral at different levels on hill sides in positions that could not be due to tilting of the hill during elevation. Also, at various sheltered points of the shores of Port Sudan and Suakin harbours, and elsewhere, the latest stage of this elevation can be traced in the form of a low cliff, standing a few yards back from the sea, fronted by a reef flat now dry land, though only a foot or two above the sea level. The cliff is undermined exactly as are those still under the influence of the waves, and even the detailed marking of the rock surface characteristic of this marine erosion remains, not yet obliterated by the flaking away of the surface through the action of the sun's heat and the cold of the clear nights, or by the filing action of the sand blasts of summer.

As explained in Chapter VIII, page 107, much of the fringing reef is really a part of the coral limestone of the coast, and its formation needs no further explanation, but it is interesting to note how greatly it varies in width in correspondence with the height of the land behind it. For instance, about Suakin it is up to 1½ miles wide, at Port Sudan only one-third of this, in correspondence with the fact that the shore about Suakin is raised scarcely two feet above sea level, whereas at Port Sudan it rises six to ten feet.

This variation is exactly what we should expect on the theory of reef formation by abrasion, the cutting down of the low-lying land involving the removal of comparatively small masses of rock and so proceeding quickly. Again, on the coast about Ankêfail (see Map, p. 139), where the land is as high as at Port Sudan, the reef is only a few yards wide, but this may be partially attributed to the shelter from waves provided by the large island Makawar.

That the differences in breadth are so marked shews that abrasion has had much more to do with the formation of the reef flats than has growth of coral, for we see no reason why this latter factor should not have operated equally well over the whole coast and tended to equalise the reefs' breadths.

But it was also explained in Chapter VII that ordinary corals cannot grow in very deep water, and as we find depths of even 200 fathoms just over the edges of these reefs we are confronted with a problem. We have explained the origin of only the surface of the ground, what lies beneath and how it came about that there was a foundation ready, within the narrow limits of depth in which corals could build, continuous through so many hundreds of miles, are the real problems. The barrier reefs, right away from land, from which they are separated by deep water, still more conspicuously need an explanation. These are the main questions of this chapter.

Barrier Reefs.

The barrier system is not a single linear reef, or line of reefs, but rather a line of areas of shallow water full of reefs of all sizes, generally more or less crescentic or ring-shaped. The details have not been surveyed, except very partially in some cases, the charts from which the map on page 126 is copied merely giving the outlines of the areas on which the reefs stand.

Some of these areas are very broad, the southernmost, Towartit, being eight miles across, their size, intricacy, and their being completely useless to all navigators but a few pearl fishers, preventing their survey within the outer borders, except in the case of that which bounds the passage to Port Sudan on the north, shewn on the map opposite. This area is obviously a continuation of the barrier system, spite of the fewness of its reefs, and the fact that over the greater part of it an average depth of 10 fathoms obtains. It is a young reef, mostly not yet grown to the surface.

Origin of Barrier Reefs.

The origin of these reefs cannot be explained by any of the theories discussed in Chapter VIII. Darwin's theory is quite inapplicable as the coast has risen continuously throughout recent geological time, and no currents could have carved out such a channel as that separating the reefs from the land, with such irregular great depths as are shewn on the maps, where, within the barrier depths over 150 fathoms are seen in proximity to soundings of only 30 to 40 fathoms, or even close alongside surface reefs.

Finally, coral growth alone, as already mentioned, could not give rise to such sheer precipices as those in which these reefs generally end.

The examination of two features of the land makes all clear at once. These are the promontories and sandstone

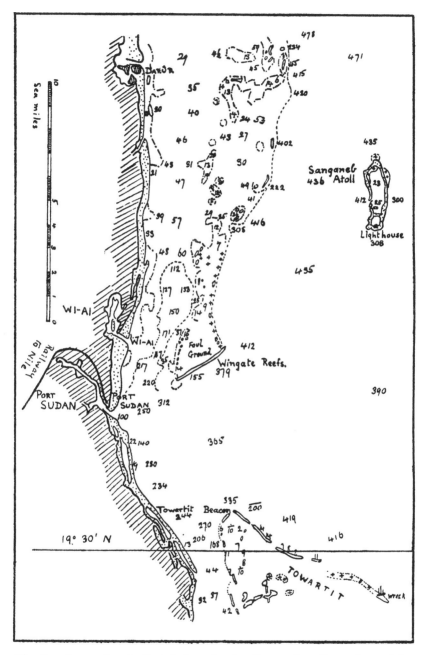

Fig. 84. Approaches to Port Sudan, shewing Sanganeb atoll, portions of the barrier reefs and fringing reef. The latter dotted.

hills, of which the Rawaya peninsula is the best example, and worth describing in some detail.

The map opposite shews that Rawaya is a large area joined by a very narrow neck to the mainland and enclosing a large bay, Khor Dongonab, about 20 fathoms deep.

Directly south of its extremity are the islands of Makawar and Mayitib, which, like Rawaya, enclose a deep basin of water (40 fathoms) on their west side, while on the east depths of 200 fathoms are found only a mile and a half from Mayitib, and 300 fathoms only three miles away, while half a mile from the islet of Shambaya the same depth occurs. In comparison the elevation of the peninsula, and even of the islands, is very trifling, and the difference of level between them and the maze of reefs which separates them absolutely negligible. Indeed

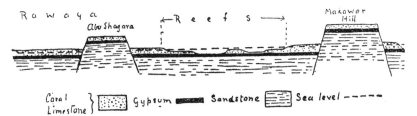

Diagram 9. Section through Rawaya and Makawar.

Rawaya is extremely low, its average being about ten feet above the sea, the areas of its two hills, Jebel Têtawib in the north, and Jebel Abu Shagara in the south, being inconsiderable, and their heights only about 40 and 127 feet. Further, an inspection of the ground shews that these hills are merely parts of the peninsula which have been thrust up to a higher level (see Diagram 9), and even on Makawar, where much of the island attains a height of over 250 feet with summits of 300 feet, the two ends and west side are low like Rawaya. In short, Rawaya, Makawar and the reefs between and about them are obviously one continuous ridge, the middle part of which is slightly lower, and, by coral growth and wave erosion, has been built up and cut down into the level area of reefs we now find there.

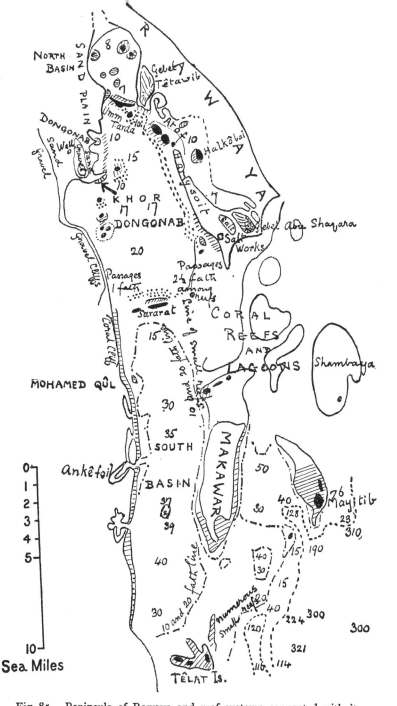

Fig. 85. Peninsula of Rawaya and reef systems connected with it

The narrow fringing reef along shore of mainland shaded as are coral beds in Khor Dongonab. Small Islands are black. Dotted areas are reefs free from coral.

—·—·—·—·— 10 (and in south basin 20) fathom line.

---------- 100 fathom line.

The conversion of such low-lying land as Rawaya into a reef maze follows at once from the action of the sea, restrained by coral growth, described in Chapter VIII, but the diagrams make the case clearer.

A is the first stage, the thin line representing the outline of a partly submarine hill range, the undulations of which are much exaggerated in the diagram. The horizontal dotted line is the sea-level, so the diagram represents one summit above the sea, an island, another submerged, and a third emerging to the right.

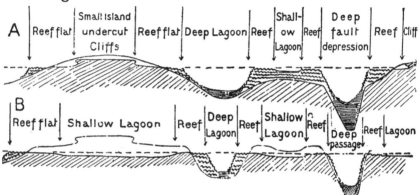

Diagram 10. Conversion of a line of low hills, partly submarine, into a maze of surface reefs

A First stage.   B after elevation and second period of abrasion.
– – – – – sea level.
〰〰〰 additions made by coral growth.
Coarse shading = remains of original hill after abrasion.
Fine shading = coral mud or sand.

In A the first summit to the left appears above water as a rounded island, which is cut down considerably and much of its area converted into reef flat, and the deep lagoon to the right is narrowed by coral growth on both this reef flat and over the next summit, as indicated by zigzag shading in the diagram.

As this second summit is at about the right depth below the surface, coral grows vigorously upon it forming a surface reef, slightly hollowed out in the middle. The third summit is like the first.

Plate XXXIX

Figs. 86 and 87. Two views on Rawaya

Upper figure in the north of the peninsula, lower near salt works in the south. Both shew one of the canal-like inlets of the sea which cut up the western side of the peninsula. In the lower one the inlet is partially cut off from the sea and the great heat has evaporated its water leaving a lake of salt. The low ground of Rawaya is shewn behind as a mere line on the horizon in the upper, but in the lower photograph the hill of Abu Shagara is included.

In B the thin line represents the final stage of A, further elevation and abrasion, with coral growth, resulting in the levelling down of islands and reefs and partial filling of the deeper lagoons as shewn by the shaded area of the diagram.

Summit No. 1 is not only cut away altogether but hollowed out into a shallow lagoon, the deep lagoon has been narrowed considerably while the ring-shaped reef on summit 2 is much as before, but has spread out and encloses a larger lagoon, thus becoming a small atoll. Summit 3 shares the fate of number one.

Now compare the outline of the original hill range in A, with the shaded line in B, and the levelling action of the sea, both upwards and downwards, is evident.

This explanation of the origin of the reefs between Makawar and Rawaya can obviously be extended to those to the south as far as the Têlat Islands, and to the whole barrier system in fact. The reefs south of Salak are similarly related to a large area of raised coral extending from the point northwards, and though there is no bay here, corresponding to Khor Dongonab, there is a large salt marsh separating this from other raised coral to the west, and formed by the filling in of a bay by blown sand. The diagrammatic map overleaf makes this clearer, and shews that on land we have continuations of both kinds of reef, the barrier being continued as the eastern coral ridge, the fringing reefs of Salak Seghir being one with the limestone on the west side of the swamp. Similarly Ras Benas to the north (lat. 24° N.) and the angle at the entrance to the Gulf of Suez, have reefs and islands in continuation of them southwards, the former being named Makawar, in this as in appearance recalling the island off Ras Rawaya.

It is now evident that the origin of both barrier and fringing reefs is identical with that of the whole coast-land, and is not to be looked for in any laws of coral growth, or marine sedimentation and abrasion, these factors having merely affected the summits of submarine hills hundreds of miles long, nearly two thousand feet high, often peculiarly narrow, and always more or less parallel to the axis of the sea-filled Rift Valley.

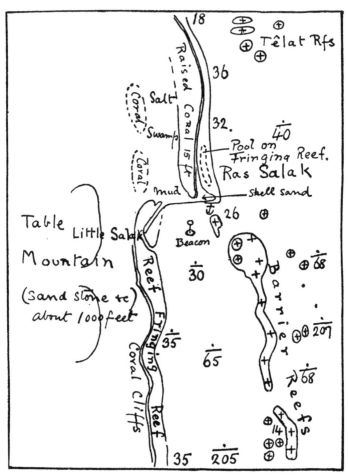

Diagram 11.   Fringing and barrier reefs in neighbourhood of Ras Salak, shewing correspondence of both systems with coral formations on land

Soundings with line and dot over mean that no bottom was found after so much line was run out.

The rocks of which these ranges are composed are laid bare in the cliffs which have resulted from the upthrusting of the hills of the Rawaya-Makawar range, and on the hill of the maritime plain.

Plate XL

Coral
←

Gypsum
←

Sandstone

Fig. 88. In a fault ravine of Abu Shagara. Cliff coral, gypsum and sandstone, the latter containing sheets of recrystallised gypsum, selenite, in every crack

I illustrate overleaf part of Jebel Têtâwib in the north part of Rawaya. It is about 40 feet high, and of this from one to six feet are occupied by the basal sandstone, a soft laminated rock generally yellow in colour, sometimes greenish or red. Next is a band, up to 20 feet thick, of gypsum, the strata of which are considerably contorted in contrast to the coral formations overlying them, which are nearly horizontal, and as usual retain the relative positions they occupied during the growth of the reef. In the south Jebel Abu Shagara is higher, 127 feet, and its cliffs, being higher, contain very much more sandstone, but are essentially the same, as are those of Jebel Makawar and Mayitib, and those of the sandstone hills of the mainland.

The sandstone ranges, coral coast-line, and barrier reefs are then three parallel repetitions of the same structure extending with great regularity along the sides of the Rift Valley from the entrance to the Gulf of Suez to Suakin, a distance of about 700 miles. Southwards of this point, as we shall see, similar structures occur, but without this extreme regularity.

Their formation is due to the opening of the Rift Valley which resulted in these sandstones[1] being thrown into a series of steps as it were along each side of the trough, as shewn on page 145. Of these we are acquainted with three, but more would probably be discovered if detailed soundings were taken from outside the barrier reefs to the narrow trough which runs down the centre of the sea and is a thousand fathoms deep.

The further history of these three steps or ridges has been as follows. We will distinguish them as numbers one, two and three, the former being the highest, the present sandstone hills and ridges of the maritime plain. The coral

[1] The gypsum often found between the sandstone and the coral was most probably formed by the drying up of a *shallow* sea which occupied the site before the Rift Valley appeared, and probably the sandstones are the sediments deposited in the same sea ; also parts of the present maritime plain were formed as the shore deposits of this ancient sea

Fig. 89. Jebel Tétâwib, in Khor Dongonab, a butt near its southern extremity, seen from its south side. The letter B is at a level about 25 feet above the foreground

A. Coral colonies, in position of growth, bedded in a mass of loose coral débris, shells, &c.
C. Hardened coral-mud. The weathered surface forms rounded masses in low relief.
D. Gypsum strata, here steeply tilted, and upturned at their ends in the piece shown in the foreground. They are much folded in other parts of the cliff.
E. Green and red shaly rock underlying and sometimes interstratified with the gypsum. It is here broken down into sand. This rock contains sheets of glass-like recrystallized gypsum.

caps on these were formed when the sea reached to the bases of the Archean hills, the sandstone range No. 1 being a line of barrier reefs off the mountainous coast-line. The mountains, then as now, were being broken down by the action of the weather, and the resulting sand and gravel was washed down into the sea as the beginning of the maritime plain.

Meanwhile organic remains were accumulating on ridge No. 2, and as elevation brought this within fifty fathoms or so of the surface, reef corals took possession and covered the summits one after another as elevation proceeded, so that

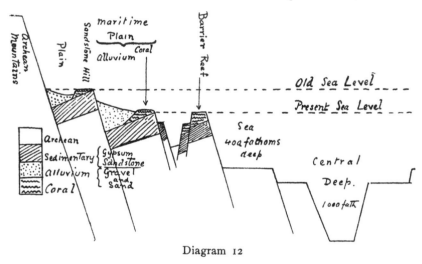

Diagram 12

when ridge No. 1 emerged from the sea altogether, and its bases were surrounded by the gravel from the hills, No. 2 was a second barrier reef out at sea.

The same process has been repeated, so that coral growth and levelling have made ridge No. 3 into the present barrier system and the maritime plain has reached the one-time barrier No. 2 and so made this the present coast-line.

During the last of these elevations a good deal of breaking and cracking of ridges Nos. 2 and 3 took place. For instance, Rawaya was originally connected with the mainland, the proof being the presence upon it of scattered pieces of Archean rock which could not possibly have reached it unless a continuous surface stretched from it to the old hills. Dongonab Bay, and with it probably other parts of the channel within the barrier system, have evidently been formed or enlarged since the maximum extension of the maritime plain. The harbours of the coast, which are so interesting in themselves as to deserve separate consideration, were formed also at this time.

Natural harbours, almost completely surrounded by land or reef, waveless in all weathers, more perfect than almost any made by man, abound throughout the length of this coast. In one part, just north of Rawaya, are ten of these strange inlets in a space of only 40 miles (see map, page 126). That of Suakin has been already described ; on entering for the first time it is hard to believe that this long parallel-sided, deep channel, bounded by reefs covered only by a foot or two of water, and then by land only the same amount above the sea, is not an artificial canal. It leads nearly straight inland for two miles, but not *quite* straight, indeed there is a bend that large steamers frequently fail to clear, and which led to the abandonment of Suakin as the Port of the Sudan.

Obviously this canal-like inlet is not the mouth of a river, past or present, for present rivers there are none, and no river, flowing over a wide plain, through loose and heterogeneous materials, could cut out such a channel, but would end in a wide shallow estuary or delta, if it formed a definite mouth at all.

The new harbour of Port Sudan is much wider both in the entrance and within, but the origin of this deep landlocked basin is equally puzzling.

The forms of all the harbours of the coast can be reduced to one plan more or less easily, that of a cross with arms parallel and at right angles to the coast-line, and are in fact formed by two cracks in the earth's surface nearly at right angles. The former arm is generally the largest, in Port Sudan it is two miles long, the other arm, which connects this with the sea and forms the shallower branch harbour,

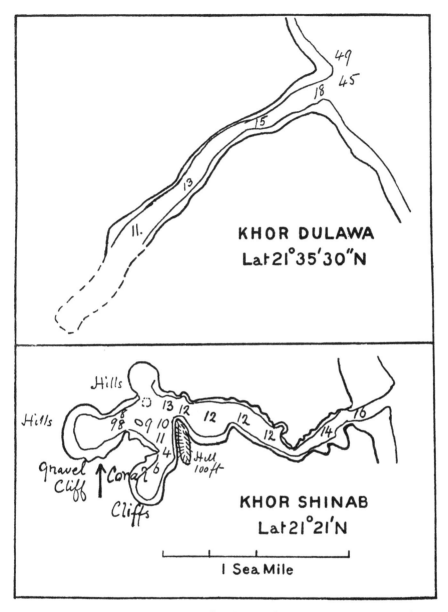

Fig. 90. Two of the canal-like "Khor" which run into the coral plain. Soundings in fathoms, note comparatively great depth of the water

The arrow in Khor Shinab indicates the point at which the material of the cliff changes from coral to gravel.

being much the shorter. The same applies to for instance Wiai, Fîjab, Salak Seghir and Ankêfail Kebir, whereas in the case of the narrower harbours, like Suakin, Arûs, Shinab and its neighbours, the arm at right angles to the sea is the longest, and the plan of the inlet is more like the conventional cross.

In Wiai, Fîjab, Salak Seghir and other harbours most of the land between the inner arm and the sea, corresponding to the East Town in Port Sudan, has been cut down

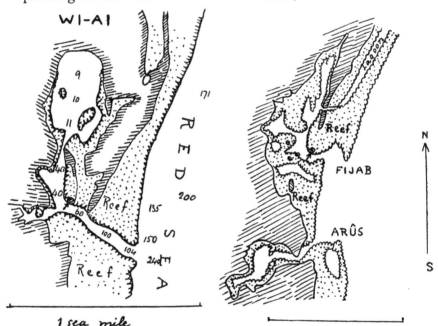

Fig. 91

and converted into reef, upon which strips of sand have accumulated to form islands in places. In all three harbours currents flowing in and out have buried the south end of this reef, next the entrance passage, in a steep sandbank (the point is marked by an arrow on the plans). As the water is too deep for convenient anchorage of small vessels, the *sambûks* run their noses on to these sandbanks, a couple of sailors walk ashore with the anchor, and they are moored for the night, as the prevailing wind is from the north.

Salak Seghir has a long narrow winding entrance, like a deep still river between reefs. Having successfully but fearfully navigated this in my launch, I found that my sailors' design was to run her on to the sandbank, *sambûk* fashion. I declined this, for my copper sheathing's sake, and was all unprepared for the fact that the passage there is about as wide as my launch is long and that the inner branch is shallow and full of humps of coral, giving me a choice of evils which I do not intend to make again. The sand lying on the reef between the inner harbour and the sea has become consolidated into sandstone in a narrow parallel-sided band, perfectly level and almost as regular as an artificial breakwater. A short length of such a formation would be striking, but this extends to nearly two miles.

These curious and most useful splits of the land have been made since the maritime plain was complete, as we saw was the case with Dongonab Bay, and, consequently, part at least of the barrier system. In some cases the innermost parts of the harbours are composed of gravel, not elevated coral. At Fîjab this is due to erosion of the coral, as shewn by rocks and islets of this material remaining on the shallows which separate the gravel cliffs from the deeper water, but in other cases the gravel bounds the actual fault.

This is well seen at Shinab, where almost the whole harbour is bounded by raised coral cliffs, but near the innermost end this is overlaid with gravel, and finally gravel replaces the coral in the most regular manner, shewing that the two materials were in perfect continuity when the split which made the harbour occurred. The north and south limbs of the crosses have been largely filled in with water and wind-carried sand ; they were originally of much greater length.

The peculiarities of the coast impress unusual methods upon those who travel along it by sea. The wave motion varies greatly; from Port Sudan to Darûr for instance the waves are much the same as on an open sea, from Darûr to Fîjab the barrier system gives considerable shelter, the vessel passing into perfect calm for short periods as she approaches near the reefs in tacking. From Shalak to the Têlat Islands is a bad bit in stormy weather, quite open sea and no possibility of anchoring anywhere in an emergency, so that vessels are often windbound at Salak[1] anchorage, waiting a fall in the wind in which to reach the next section of the barrier system.

To travel by night is obviously impossible, the navigation of a boat, even among well-known reefs, when moonlight seems bright as day, is an experience once tried never repeated, without urgent cause. Even when the sun is low it is extremely difficult to see one's way, though a good native pilot sees indications of reefs where all is a white glare to even an experienced Englishman. Consequently it is the invariable custom to get into the nearest harbour about four o'clock in the afternoon, and if the coast were not thus liberally provided, the natives' travel by sea would be nearly impossible. The start is early next morning, between 2 a.m. and 4 a.m. according to the wind and the distance of the reefs. If the wind is fairly off shore, so that the neighbourhood of reefs will not be reached for some time, the start is early and the sail is hoisted in a strange silence, the sleepy sailors, on these occasions only, omitting their shouts and chants, and the vessel slips out of harbour like a slowly-gliding ghost.

As already remarked the formation we have described is that of almost the whole Red Sea, but south of Suakin it loses the regularity that is so noticeable northwards. The area marked on the map (p. 126) as "Suakin Archipelago" consists of innumerable small reefs, shoals and islets, the water between being of very irregular depth, three hundred fathoms being found close alongside surface reefs. Opposite Trinkitat the water shoals gradually, only 30 to 40 fathoms being found as far as 45 miles from land. The shore itself is extremely low and sandstone hills are absent. The area marked Shubuk, south of Suakin, shewn on the map enclosed by a thin semi-circular line on the north and east sides and by the land on the

---

[1] The forms Salak and Shalak are both used by the natives.

west and south, has a very remarkable structure. An area of
100 square miles is enclosed by a regular and unbroken reef,
indicated by the above curved line, the space within being
a most intricate maze of reefs with comparatively deep canal-
like passages between them. In the south are broader passages
and some islets of elevated coral. The bounding reef is extremely regular and, on its eastern side, unbroken. It consists
of a steep slope and precipice of growing coral up to near the
surface, when the slope becomes very gradual and forms a
nearly smooth surface of stunted corals with grey *Xenia*.
This extends to among the breakers, above which is a band
of gravel formed of broken and wave-rounded pieces of coral.
Within is sand, and the coral capped sandbanks of the
labyrinth. Landwards the ground is for miles so low and
so much broken into by salt lagoons and marshes that a
definite coast-line can scarcely be said to exist.

This is the remains of an old delta of the Khor Baraka,
a river which rises in the Abyssinian highlands, but which
nowadays never reaches the sea. Its floods come down on
to the maritime plain at Tokar, where, spreading over a considerable area, they render possible the growth of cotton and
other crops in the fine soil they leave soaked with water.
Tokar is thus the one fruitful spot of any size on the whole
Red Sea coast, but its character of fertile oasis is but short-
lived. When the crops are gathered even the dry cotton
stalks must be removed lest they should collect the sand,
which, every day of the summer, is carried over them by
burning gales, and so would convert the fertile ground into
barren sandhills.

As it is, at any rate at present, impossible to predict these
floods the seed must be sown after each, even though it
frequently happens that another flood comes down and carries
it all away. The seed must then be patiently re-sown, and
that left by the last flood will grow and bear. In the old days,
before man was there to make any use of it, the Baraka formed
a regular delta, subject to yearly floods, a miniature Egypt.

The growth of coral in this neighbourhood would then be impossible, the shifting sand, muddy and freshened water rendering its life impossible.

Now when the rainfall decreased so that for the greater part of the year no freshwater stream entered the sea, and the materials of the edges of the delta became stationary, coral growth arose here and there, forming a fringing reef, the extension of which seawards must have been exceptionally rapid in this gradually shelving water. There was then an elevation of the sea-bottom, here comparatively slight, and the sea began to cut into the raised coral, carving it out into islets, surface reefs, tidal channels and lagoons.

At the seaward edge of the reefs, the coral in the purer water could continue as it is doing now, a rapid and continuous growth, the uniformity of the conditions producing the remarkable unbroken reef already described. The disintegrating forces described in Chapter VIII break the inner side of the reef into sandy flats and pools, but the extension of these pools into wider spaces and continuous channels makes coral growth again possible in the shallows on their banks, so that all the inner sandbanks and rocks are capped with live corals which prevents their further demolition and gives the steep-sided canal-like form to the passages between them.

Living Reefs.

In detail the living reefs of the Red Sea are characterised by (1) their luxuriant growth of coral, (2) the absence of large stones or "negro-heads" along their edges, (3) their frequently crescentic or circular forms. There are remarkably few points on the coast where coral is not growing in abundance, and at the edges of reefs in the open sea its luxuriance is wonderful. Even at the inner ends of the canal-like harbours, where the water is stagnant and dirty, scattered colonies are found. The absence of rivers probably favours these growths, but even so the floods bring fresh water into the harbours occasionally, and colour their waters a deep red brown, like the Nile in flood, for several days together once or twice a year. The absence of strong currents carrying mud is another factor; where such occur, in Khor Dongonab, the vertical sided coral reefs give place to sloping bottoms of rock covered with stones formed by the growth of lithothamnia—stony seaweeds—but I only know this one place where these conditions prevail.

There are no stones of any size on the edges of the reefs, nothing but a few pieces of coral, a foot or so in diameter at most, project above lowest water level. It would decrease the danger of navigation in dead calm weather, which at present, except in frequented places, is considerable, if larger stones, such as the "negro-heads" of some reefs, were present at intervals. As in most cases these larger masses are the remains of former land and are not, as sometimes stated, fragments of the living reef thrown up by storms, one cannot expect their presence here, where the reef edge has grown up *in situ*. But even large boulders such as form the "hurricane beach" of Pacific atolls, and are cast up by storms in profusion on the reefs of Queensland, are not found here. There is plenty of strong wind in the Red Sea, but the strongest of all, the hot winds of summer, blow off land and do not extend far to sea and such vast breakers, up to 40 feet high, as are recorded of the Pacific, never occur. The reef edge above the precipice consists of a slope of stunted coral which above water-level changes to a gravel of coral fragments coated with lithothamnia; within is sand, generally with bands of seaweeds and marine flowering plants (grass-like in appearance) on the shallows, with muddy pools and channels a fathom or two deep. The edge is higher than the rest, but does not appear continuously above lowest water-level. Reefs not exposed to the waves have not this definite edge, the platform being covered with two or three feet of water in which stand separate coral colonies, numerous at the edge, rarer within towards the lagoon.

The crescentic or circular forms of isolated reefs is very far from being a peculiarity of the Red Sea, but is worth while mentioning as bearing on the formation of the lagoons of atolls on the larger scale.   From the smallest to the largest these reefs shew a hollowing out in the centre, where the reef material, not being protected by living matter, is exposed to the destructive influences detailed in Chapter VIII.

There are some reefs in the Red Sea quite of the Atoll form, of which the largest is Sanganeb, the plan of which, on the map on page 137, is sufficiently explanatory.   Another is Tella Tella Seghir, which is elevated to 40 feet above sea-level, and consists of a ring of high ground enclosing a depression, once a lagoon though its floor is now a little above sea-level.   The elevation of this ring-shaped reef has been at least two stages, the lagoon having contained water to about one-third of its depth comparatively recently, since a line of undermined cliffs occurs at this level.   The *Admiralty Pilot* remarks that the edge of the ridge bears numerous cairns.   Some of these are artificial I am told, but those I examined were large coral colonies, in the position in which they grew, left exposed by the removal of the softer stuff in which they were embedded. One example of the coral genus *Mussa* was especially conspicuous, as much so as the corals illustrated on Plate XXXVII on the top of Jebel Têtâwib.

Summary of Geological History of the Red Sea.

(1) There was originally a *shallow* sea covering the space between the high mountains of both sides of the present Red Sea.   In this sea were laid down sandy and gravelly sediments, and limestones were formed which are now found in the sandstone hills of the maritime plain, &c.

The gypsum beds found here are the result of the drying up of the water of this shallow sea.

(2) The beds of rock thus formed were broken up by the sinking in of a long strip of the earth's crust forming

the Rift Valley, which extends from Jordan to Tanganyika. Part of this valley was filled by sea water and became the Red Sea.

(3) There have been three successive systems of barrier reefs along the Red Sea coast, which by continual uplift have become,

(*a*) A range of sandstone hills rising from the alluvial maritime plain.

(*b*) A fringe of limestone along the present coast-line.

(*c*) The present barrier system.

(4) These three ridges were formed by the faulting of sedimentary rocks which overlay the bases of the Archean hills at the time of the great movement which opened the Red Sea section of the Great Rift Valley.

(5) The northern ends of several sections of the present barrier reefs are elevated above sea-level, and examination of these, and of the hills of the maritime plain, enable us to reach the above conclusions.

(6) At the same time Rawaya gives evidence of a seaward movement as well as uplift, Khor Dongonab and some at least of the channel within the barrier reefs being recent fault depressions, not merely an anticlinal fold formed at the opening of the Rift Valley.

The harbours and other fissures in the coral limestones, &c. of both coast-land and of the barrier reefs are due to the same secondary faulting.

(7) The maritime plain had its maximum seaward extension after the growth of coral on the second and third barriers. Owing to elevation nothing has been added to its seaward slopes since the formation of the features of the present coast-line by secondary faulting.

(8) The filling in of valleys and the completion of the connection of the second barrier with the maritime plain has been largely due to blown sand. The process is continuing, e.g. an extensive plain near Dongonab shews perfect uniformity in its formation.

INDEX

Plate II

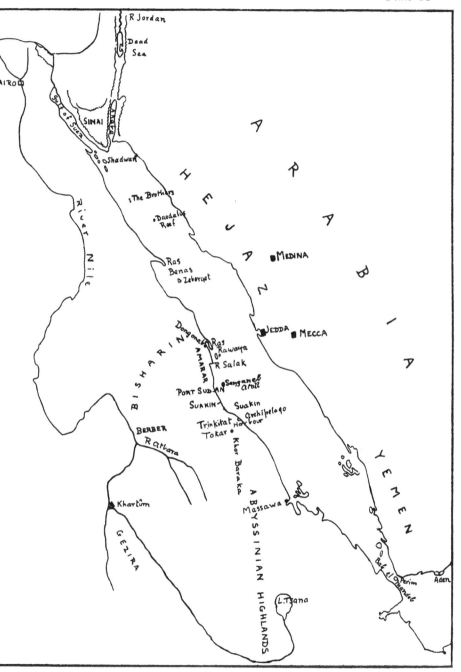

Fig. 2. Map of Red Sea